365 Easy Pasta Recipes

Delicious, versatile
recipes for easy meals

HINKLER
BOOKS

Cover by Nancy Bohanan
Pre-press by Graphic Print Group

365 Easy Pasta Recipes
Published in 2009 by Hinkler Books Pty Ltd
45–55 Fairchild Street
Heatherton VIC 3202 Australia
www.hinklerbooks.com

© Cookbook Resources, LLC 2008

10 9 8 7 6 5 4 3 2
14 13 12 11 10

ISBN: 978 1 7418 3131 3
Printed and bound in China

Introduction

365 Easy Pasta Recipes is all about one of the easiest, no-fail foods available – pasta. Pasta is a classic family favourite and these 365 recipes feature it in every size and interesting shape. Pasta is quick and simple to prepare, making it an easy meal on weeknights or weekends.

Increasingly, we have come to realise just how important mealtime together is to a family. Bonds are built and relationships are strengthened as healthy values and habits are instilled.

365 Easy Pasta Recipes makes it easy to plan, to cook and to serve delicious dishes to family and friends. All the ingredients are readily available in your own pantry, refrigerator or at your local supermarket.

Add a simple salad or a purchased dessert and consider everyone's favourite, garlic bread, as an accompaniment.

Cooking is one of life's simple pleasures. And these recipes make it easy to enjoy quality time with people you care about.

Contents

Starters & Soups 7

*Delicious starters for any meal, many are meals in themselves.
Soups and stews are always warm gifts from the heart.*

Scrumptious Salads 35

*Veggie salads and meat salads that can be a complete meal are
filling, tasty and easy.*

Pasta with Beef 75

*Appetising and hearty recipes with beef at the centre make pasta
a family favourite.*

Pasta with Chicken 121

*Chicken is so versatile and when you add pasta, it's great for
everyday meals – and entertaining.*

Contents

Dedication

With a mission of helping you bring family and friends to the table, this book aims to make family meals and cooking for friends simple, easy and delicious.

We recognise the importance of a meal together as a means of building family bonds with memories and traditions that will be treasured for a lifetime. It is an opportunity to sit down with each other and share more than food.

This cookbook is dedicated with gratitude and respect to all those who show their love with homecooked meals, bringing family and friends to the table.

More and more statistical studies are finding that family meals play a significant role in childhood development. Children who eat with their families four or more nights per week are healthier, attain higher marks at school, score higher on aptitude tests and are less likely to have problems with drugs.

Starters
& Soups

Delicious starters for any meal, many are meals in themselves. Soups and stews are always warm gifts from the heart.

Starters & Soups Contents

Pasta is available in a number of colours and flavours to add both taste and attractiveness to your dish. Pasta colourata *is the Italian term and includes green (spinach) or* pasta verde, *red (carrot) or* pasta rossa, *purple (tomato or beetroot) or* pasta viola, *and a number of other flavours and colours.*

Appetising Tortellinis

⅓ cup (75 ml) red wine vinegar
¾ cup (175 ml) olive oil
1 tablespoon (15 ml) Dijon-style
    mustard
1 teaspoon minced garlic
1 teaspoon sugar
570 g (20 ounces) refrigerated
    chicken-filled tortellini pasta
1 cup (130 g) whole, pitted black
    olives
230 g (8 ounces) mozzarella cheese,
    cubed
1 red capsicum, seeded,
    julienned
1 200-g (7-ounce) can baby corn,
    drained
2 tablespoons (10 g) chopped
    fresh parsley

- To make marinade, combine vinegar, olive oil, mustard, garlic, sugar and a little salt and pepper in large bowl.

- Cook pasta in saucepan according to package directions; drain and rinse in cold water. Place tortellini in large bowl and add olives, cheese, capsicum and baby corn.

- Pour marinade over pasta mixture and refrigerate for at least 1 or 2 hours. When ready to serve, sprinkle with chopped parsley and serve with toothpicks. Serves 12.

Seafood in the Shell

340 g (12 ounces) lumache
    (large pasta shells)
460 g (16 ounces) cream cheese,
    softened
⅓ cup (75 g) mayonnaise
1 tablespoon (15 ml) lemon
    juice
2 tablespoons (25 g) sugar
1 teaspoon seasoned salt
455 g (16 ounces) imitation
    crabmeat,
    finely flaked
1 170-g (6-ounce) can tuna,
    drained, flaked
1 stick celery, finely diced

- Cook 36 jumbo pasta shells in saucepan until al dente. Drain and place on large sheet of baking paper.

- Beat cream cheese, mayonnaise, lemon juice, sugar, seasoned salt and ½ teaspoon black pepper in mixing bowl until creamy and smooth. Fold in crabmeat, tuna and celery; mix until they blend well.

- Stuff cream cheese-tuna mixture into jumbo pasta shells, cover and refrigerate for at least 2 hours before serving. Serves 6.

TIP: These shells can be served as a side dish or as a starter.

Appetiser Bites

230 g (8 ounces) conchiglie
    pasta
1 340-g (12-ounce) can tuna,
    drained, flaked
1 stick celery, finely diced
2 tablespoons (20 g) diced
    green capsicum
115 g (4 ounces) roasted red
    capsicum, chopped
¼ cup (30 g) finely chopped
    pecans
¾–1 cup (170–225 g) mayonnaise

- Cook pasta in saucepan until al
  dente. Drain and rinse in cold
  water; drain again. Combine tuna,
  celery, capsicum, roasted red
  capsicum and pecans with a little
  salt and pepper in medium bowl.
  Stir in ¾ (170 g) cup mayonnaise
  and add additional ¼ cup (55 g)
  mayonnaise if mixture needs to be
  creamier for stuffing.

- Carefully stuff the pasta
  and serve as appetisers.
  Serves 6 to 12.

Mexican-Style Minestrone Soup

230 g (8 ounces) elbow pasta
1 455-g (16-ounce) jar thick-
    and-chunky salsa
1 425-g (15-ounce) can borlotti
    beans with liquid
1 teaspoon paprika
1 teaspoon ground cumin
1 teaspoon minced garlic
230 g (8 ounces) shredded chedder
    cheese
2 medium zucchini, cut in half
    lengthwise, sliced
1 200-g (7-ounce) can corn kernels

- Cook pasta in saucepan according
  to package directions. Drain and set
  aside.

- Combine all ingredients, except
  cheese and cooked pasta, in large
  saucepan with 1 cup (250 ml)
  water. Bring to a boil, reduce heat
  and simmer for 8 minutes stirring
  often.

- Stir in pasta, and top each serving
  with cheese. Serves 6.

Chickpea Soup

2 tablespoons (30 ml) olive oil
1 brown onion, chopped
1 capsicum, chopped
2 teaspoons minced
    garlic
½ teaspoon dried sage
1 425-g (15-ounce) can
    stewed tomatoes
1 litre (28 ounces) carton vegetable
    stock
1 425-g (15-ounce) can
    chickpeas, drained
½ cup (55 g) elbow macaroni
    pasta tubes
1 teaspoon Italian
    seasoning
145 g (5 ounces) grated parmesan
    cheese

- Combine olive oil, onions and capsicums, and garlic in soup pot and cook, stirring often on medium heat for 5 minutes or until onions are translucent. Stir in sage, tomatoes, vegetable stock, chickpeas and a little salt and pepper and cook for 10 minutes.

- Stir in pasta and Italian seasoning and cook for about 15 minutes or until pasta is al dente (tender, but not overdone). Place about 1 heaped tablespoon parmesan cheese over each serving. Serves 4 to 6.

Italian Minestrone

1 brown onion, chopped
1 capsicum, chopped
3 sticks celery, chopped
2 teaspoons minced garlic
¼ cup (60 g) butter
2 425-g (15-ounce) cans diced
    tomatoes
1 teaspoon dried oregano
1 teaspoon dried basil
1 litre (28 ounces) carton beef stock
2 425-g (15-ounce) cans kidney
    beans, drained
2 medium zucchini, cut
    in half lengthwise, sliced
1 cup (105 g) elbow macaroni
    pasta tubes

- Sauté onion and capsicum, celery and garlic in butter for about 2 minutes in soup pot. Add tomatoes, oregano, basil and a little salt and pepper. Boil, reduce heat and simmer for 15 minutes, stirring occasionally.

- Stir in beef stock, beans, zucchini, pasta and boil. Reduce heat and simmer for additional 15 minutes or until pasta is tender. Serves 8.

Gomito maccheroni *is the Italian for elbow macaroni.*

Main Dish Minestrone Soup

1 tablespoon (15 ml) olive oil
1 onion, chopped
2 teaspoons minced garlic
2 425-g (15-ounce) cans
   Italian stewed tomatoes
280 g (10 ounces) frozen chopped
   spinach, thawed, drained
1 230-g (8-ounce) can sliced
   carrots, drained
1 cup (125 g) coarsely chopped
   zucchini
1 small potato, peeled, cubed
2 sticks celery, sliced
1 cup (10 ounces) beef stock

1 teaspoon dried basil
1 teaspoon dried oregano
½ cup (40 g) conchiglie or
   maruzze pasta shells
1 425-g (15-ounce) can
   cannellini beans, drained

- Heat oil in soup pot and cook onion and garlic for 3 minutes. Add tomatoes, spinach, carrots, zucchini, potato, celery, stock, basil, oregano and 7 cups (1.6 L) water.

- Bring to a boil and simmer for 15 minutes.

- Add pasta and beans to soup mixture and cook over medium heat for 10 to 12 minutes or until pasta is tender. Serves 6 to 8.

Conchiglie pasta is shell-shaped. It's a popular and fun pasta that comes in various sizes from small ones for soup to medium for salads and casseroles to large ones that can be stuffed and baked.

Pasta-Veggie Soup

2 yellow squash, chopped
2 zucchini, sliced
280 g (10 ounces) frozen whole corn
    kernels, thawed
1 red capsicum, chopped
1 425-g (15-ounce) can stewed
    tomatoes
1 teaspoon Italian seasoning
2 teaspoons dried oregano
1 litre (28 ounces) carton beef
    stock
¾ cup (180 ml) gnocchi
Shredded mozzarella cheese

- Combine squash, zucchini, corn, capsicum, tomatoes, Italian seasoning, oregano, beef stock and 2 cups (500 ml) water in 6-L (6-quart) slow cooker.

- Cover and cook on low for 6 to 7 hours.

- Add pasta and cook for additional 30 to 45 minutes or until pasta is tender.

- Garnish with a sprinkle of shredded mozzarella cheese on each bowl of soup. Serves 4 to 5.

Veggie and Tortellini Soup

2 tablespoons (30 g) butter
2 sticks celery, sliced
1 carrot, peeled, sliced
1 onion, chopped
1 cup (150 g) chopped green
    capsicum
1 teaspoon minced garlic
1 litre (28 ounces) chicken stock
340 g (12 ounces) dried cheese-filled
    tortellini pasta
1 tablespoon (15 ml) chopped
    fresh parsley
½ cup (50 g) grated parmesan
    cheese

- Melt butter in large soup pot over medium heat. Cook celery, carrot, onion, capsicum, garlic and stock for about 6 minutes or until vegetables are tender but crisp.

- Stir in pasta and parsley, cover and cook for about 20 minutes, stirring occasionally or until pasta is tender. Sprinkle a little parmesan cheese over each serving. Serves 6.

TIP: This soup is good without adding any meat, but if you like you could add chicken or ham to make a heavier soup.

Pasta rigate refers to the pasta with ridges. The little grooves and sticks help sauce cling to these pastas.

Pizza Soup

3 280-g (10-ounce) cans
   condensed tomato soup
1 280-g (10-ounce) can
   French onion soup
2 teaspoons Italian seasoning
¾ cup (80 g) gnocchi
1½ cups (175 g) shredded
   mozzarella cheese

- Place tomato soup, French onion soup, Italian seasoning and 1½ soup cans water in 4 to 5-L (4 to 5-quart) slow cooker. Turn heat setting to high and cook 1 hour or until mixture is hot.

- Add pasta and cook for 1 hour 30 minutes to 2 hours or until pasta is done. Stir several times to keep pasta from sticking to bottom of slow cooker. Turn heat off, add mozzarella cheese and stir until cheese melts. Serves 4.

TIP: *For a special way to serve this soup, sprinkle some fried onions over top of each serving.*

Warm-Your-Soul Soup

1.25 litres (42 ounces) chicken
   stock
1 280-g (10-ounce) can Italian
   stewed tomatoes with liquid
½ cup (80 g) chopped onion
¾ cup (75 g) chopped celery
170 g (6 ounces) fettuccini
   (medium egg noodles)

- Combine chicken stock, tomatoes, onion and celery in large soup pot. Boil and simmer until onion and celery are almost done.

- Add pasta and cook until al dente (firm but tender). Season with a little salt and pepper. Serves 4.

Beef and Pasta Soup

680 g (1½ pounds) lean minced
    beef
1 onion, chopped
2 425-g (15-ounce) cans mixed
    vegetables, drained
2 425-g (15-ounce) cans
    Italian stewed tomatoes
1 litre (28 ounces) beef stock
1 teaspoon dried oregano
1 cup (105 g) fettuccini
    (medium egg noodles) pasta

- Brown and cook beef in frypan until no longer pink and transfer to slow cooker.

- Add onion, mixed vegetables, stewed tomatoes, beef stock and oregano.

- Cover and cook on low for 4 to 5 hours.

- Cook pasta in saucepan according to package direction.

- Add pasta to slow cooker and cook for 30 minutes. Serves 4 to 6.

Beef-Noodle Soup

455 g (1 pound) lean minced beef
1.4-L (46-ounce) can
    vegetable juice
30 g (1 ounce) onion soup mix
85 g (3 ounces) beef-flavoured
    ramen noodles
455 g (16 ounces) frozen
    broccoli-cauliflower mixture,
    thawed

- Cook beef in large saucepan over medium heat until no longer pink and drain. Stir in vegetable juice, soup mix, noodle seasoning, broccoli and cauliflowers and bring to a boil.

- Reduce heat and simmer, for 6 minutes or until vegetables are tender. Return to boil and stir in noodles.

- Cook for 3 minutes or until noodles are tender and serve hot. Serves 6.

Beefy Vegetable Soup

455 g (1 pound) lean minced beef
1 1.4-L (46-ounce) can
    vegetable juice
30 g (1 ounce) packet mushroom
    soup mix
85 g (3 ounces) beef-flavoured
    ramen noodles
455 g (16 ounces) frozen
    mixed vegetables

- Cook beef in large soup pot over medium heat until no longer pink. Drain. Stir in vegetable juice, soup mix, contents of noodle seasoning packet and mixed vegetables.

- Heat mixture to boiling, reduce heat and simmer for 6 minutes or until vegetables are tender but crisp. Return to boiling, stir in noodles and cook for 3 minutes. Serves 6.

Italian Beefy Veggie Soup

455 g (1 pound) lean minced beef
2 teaspoons minced garlic
2 425-g (15-ounce) cans
    Italian stewed tomatoes
1 litre (28 ounces) beef stock
2 teaspoons Italian seasoning
455 g (16 ounces) frozen mixed
    vegetables
⅓ cup (35 g) macaroni (tube)
    pasta
230 g (8 ounces) shredded
    mozzarella cheese

- Cook beef and garlic in large soup pot for 5 minutes. Stir in tomatoes, stock, 1 cup (250 ml) water, Italian seasoning, mixed vegetables, pasta and a little salt and pepper.

- Boil, reduce heat and simmer for 10 to 15 minutes or until pasta is tender.

- Ladle into individual serving bowls and sprinkle several tablespoons cheese over top of soup. Serves 4.

Mother's Beef-Veggie Soup

455 g (1 pound) lean minced
    beef
30 g (1 ounce) onion soup mix
1 litre (28 ounces) beef stock
2 425-g (15-ounce) cans
    stewed tomatoes
2 425-g (15-ounce) cans mixed
    vegetables with liquid
1 cup (105 g) macaroni (tube)
    pasta

- Brown beef in soup pot over high
  heat and drain. Reduce heat to
  medium and add soup mix, stock,
  tomatoes, mixed vegetables and
  1 cup (250 ml) water and cook for
  5 minutes.

- Stir in pasta and cook for
  15 minutes or until pasta is tender,
  stirring occasionally. Serves 6.

Rewards with Italian Soup

455 g (1 pound) lean minced beef
2 green capsicums,
    seeded, coarsely chopped
1 large onion, coarsely chopped
½ cup (35 g) shredded carrot
2 teaspoons minced garlic
1 litre (28 ounces) carton
    beef stock
2 425-g (15-ounce) cans Italian
    stewed tomatoes
1 tablespoon (15 ml) sugar
1 tablespoon (15 ml) Italian
    seasoning
230 g (8 ounces) conchiglie
    (medium shells) pasta

- Cook beef, capsicums, onion, carrot
  and garlic in large soup pot over
  medium heat until beef is no longer
  pink; drain.

- Add beef stock, 4 cups (1 L) water,
  stewed tomatoes, sugar, Italian
  seasoning and a little salt and pepper.
  Bring to the boil, stir in pasta, reduce
  heat to medium and cook for about
  15 minutes. Serves 10.

Soup in a Snap

455 g (1 pound) lean minced beef
85 g (3 ounces) Oriental noodles
      with beef flavour
1 litre (28 ounces) carton
      beef stock
455 g (16 ounces) frozen
      mixed vegetables
2 sticks celery, sliced
2 tablespoons (30 ml) soy sauce

- Brown beef in frypan on medium-high heat, drain and set aside.

- Break up noodles, add seasoning packet, beef stock, 1 cup (250 ml) water, mixed vegetables, celery and soy sauce in soup pot. Bring to a boil, stir in minced beef and simmer for 10 to 15 minutes or until vegetables are tender. Serves 6 to 8.

Country-Style Beefy Soup

680 g (1½ pounds) lean minced
      beef
1 onion, chopped
1 capsicum, chopped
2 teaspoons minced garlic
1 litre (28 ounces) carton
      beef stock
2 425-g (15-ounce) cans
      Italian stewed tomatoes
3 teaspoons Italian seasoning
1½ cups (160 g) macaroni (tube)
      pasta
Shredded cheddar cheese

- Brown and cook beef, onion, capsicums and garlic in soup pot on medium heat. Add beef stock, 2 cups (500 ml) water, stewed tomatoes and Italian seasoning and boil for 2 minutes.

- Add pasta and cook, stirring occasionally on medium heat for about 15 minutes. When serving, sprinkle cheese over each serving. Serves 6.

Chunky Beefy Pasta Soup

455 g (1 pound) beef round steak,
    cubed
1 onion, chopped
2 sticks celery, sliced
1 tablespoon (15 ml) olive oil
1 tablespoon (15 ml) paprika
½ teaspoon dried oregano
1 425-g (15-ounce) can
    stewed tomatoes
1 litre (28 ounces) beef stock
115 g (8 ounces) fettuccini
    (medium egg noodles) pasta
1 green capsicum,
    seeded, chopped

- Cook and stir cubed steak, onion and celery in soup pot with oil for 15 minutes or until beef browns.

- Stir in 2 cups (500 ml) water, 1 teaspoon salt, paprika, oregano, stewed tomatoes and beef stock. Boil, reduce heat and simmer for 1 hour 30 minutes to 2 hours or until beef is tender.

- Stir in pasta and capsicum and heat to boiling. Reduce heat and simmer for 10 to 15 minutes or until pasta is tender. Serves 4.

Fettuccini, *a stickbon pasta, is the Italian name for 'little stickbons'.*

Spaghetti Soup

**200 g (7 ounces) spaghetti pasta,
broken**
**510 g (18 ounces) frozen, cooked
meatballs, thawed**
**1 795-g (28-ounce) jar
spaghetti sauce**
**1 425-g (15-ounce) can
stewed tomatoes**
1 tablespoon (15 ml) paprika

- Cook pasta in soup pot with 2 L
(2 quarts) boiling water and a little
salt for about 6 minutes (no need to
drain).

- When pasta is done, add meatballs,
spaghetti sauce, paprika and stewed
tomatoes and cook until mixture
heats through. Serves 6.

*TIP: If you want to garnish each
soup bowl, sprinkle with
2 tablespoons (15 g) mozzarella
cheese or whatever cheese you
have in the refrigerator.*

Chicken-Noodle Soup

**85 g (3 ounces) chicken-flavoured
ramen noodles, broken**
**280 g (10 ounces) frozen
green peas, thawed**
**1 115-g (4-ounce) can sliced
mushrooms, drained**
**3 cups (420 g) cooked, cubed
chicken**

- Heat 2¼ cups (560 ml) water in
large saucepan to boiling. Add
noodles, contents of seasoning
packet and peas. Heat to boiling,
reduce heat to medium and cook for
about 5 minutes.

- Stir in mushrooms and chicken
and continue cooking over low
heat until all ingredients are hot.
To serve, spoon into soup bowls.
Serves 6 to 8.

Plum Good Soup

2 tablespoons (30 ml) olive oil
340 g (¾ pound) beef round steak,
    cubed
1 onion, chopped
2 sticks celery, chopped
2 teaspoons minced garlic
1 litre (32 ounces) carton
    beef stock
1 230-g (8-ounce) can
    tomato puree
1 280-g (10-ounce) can tomatoes
2 green chillies seeded, chopped
2 teaspoons Italian seasoning
280 g (10 ounces) frozen Italian
    green beans
⅔ cup (50 g) orzo or pastina (tiny)
    pasta
Grated parmesan cheese

- Heat oil in soup pot over medium-high heat. Add beef, onion, celery and garlic. Cook and stir until meat is crusty brown and onion and celery are tender.

- Stir in beef stock, tomato puree, tomatoes, green chillies and Italian seasoning. Simmer for 45 minutes.

- Add green beans, pasta and a little salt and pepper; bring to a boil. Cook and stir often for 5 minutes. Sprinkle 1 tablespoon (15 ml) parmesan cheese over top of each serving. Serves 6 to 8.

Tiny pastas like orzo are good to use in soups.

Chicken-Pasta Soup

680 g (1½ pounds) boneless,
skinless chicken thighs, cubed
1 onion, chopped
3 carrots, sliced
½ cup (65 g) halved, pitted
black olives
1 teaspoon minced garlic
1.25 litre (32 ounces) carton
chicken stock
1 425-g (15-ounce) can Italian
stewed tomatoes
1 teaspoon Italian seasoning
½ cup (55 g) gnocchi
Parmesan cheese

- Combine all ingredients in slow cooker except gnocchi and parmesan cheese.

- Cover and cook on low for 8 to 9 hours. About 30 minutes before serving, add pasta and stir.

- Increase heat to high and cook for additional 20 to 30 minutes. Garnish with parmesan cheese. Serves 6 to 8.

Feel-Better Chicken-Noodle Soup

85 g (3 ounces) chicken-flavoured
ramen noodles, broken
280 g (10 ounces) frozen green peas,
thawed
2 teaspoons butter
1 115-g (4-ounce) can sliced
mushrooms, drained
3 cups (420 g) cooked,
cubed chicken

- Heat 2¼ cups (540 ml) water in large saucepan to boiling.

- Add noodles, contents of seasoning packet, peas and butter. Heat to boiling, reduce heat to medium and cook about 5 minutes.

- Stir in mushrooms and chicken and continue cooking over low heat until all ingredients heat through. To serve, spoon into serving bowls. Serves 6.

Old-Fashioned Chicken-Pasta Soup

1.3 kg–1.8 kg (3–4 pound)
    whole chicken
1 carrot, chopped
2 sticks celery with leaves, chopped
½–¾ cup (95–145 g) tagliatelle
    (thin egg noodles) pasta,
    cooked

- Wash whole chicken and giblets and put in large soup pot. Add 7 to 8 cups (1.6 to 2 L) water, carrot and celery and bring to a boil. Reduce heat and simmer, partially covered, for 45 minutes to 1 hour or until meat is tender.

- Remove chicken from soup pot and cool. Continue simmering and spoon off fat from top of liquid when needed.

- Bone chicken and put all bones and skin back into soup pot. Continue to simmer for 3 to 4 hours. Turn heat off and strain chicken stock in large bowl. Add chopped chicken and cooked pasta. Add a little salt and pepper. Serves 4.

Oriental Chicken-Noodle Soup

85 g (3 ounces) chicken-flavoured
    ramen noodles
1 roast chicken, boned,
    skinned, cubed
2 medium stalks bok choy
    with leaves, thinly sliced
1 230-g (8-ounce) can
    sliced carrots, drained
1 red capsicum, seeded,
    chopped

- Break apart noodles, place in 3 cups (750 ml) water and heat in soup pot. Stir in chicken, bok choy, carrots and capsicum.

- Boil, reduce heat and simmer for 3 minutes; stir occasionally. Stir in flavour packet from noodles and serve immediately. Serves 6.

Quick Chicken-Pasta Soup

1 litre (28 ounces) chicken
    stock
2 boneless, skinless
    chicken breast halves, cubed
1 230-g (8-ounce) can sliced
    carrots, drained
2 sticks celery, sliced
115 g (4 ounces) fettuccini (medium
    egg noodles) pasta

- Combine stock, chicken, carrots, celery and generous dash of pepper in large saucepan. Boil and cook for 3 minutes.

- Stir in pasta, reduce heat and cook for 10 minutes or until noodles are done; stir often. Serves 4.

Turkey and Mushroom Soup

*Another great way to use
leftover chicken or turkey.*

2 cups (145 g) sliced shitake
    mushrooms
2 sticks celery, sliced
1 small onion, chopped
2 tablespoons (30 g) butter
1 425-g (15-ounce) can
    sliced carrots, drained
1 litre (28 ounces) chicken stock
½ cup (55 g) orzo (tiny) pasta
2 cups (280 g) cooked, chopped
    turkey or chicken

- Sauté mushrooms, celery and onion with butter in frypan.

- Transfer to slow cooker and add carrots, stock, pasta and turkey. (Do not use smoked turkey.)

- Cover and cook on low for 2 to 3 hours or on high for 1 to 2 hours. Serves 4 to 6.

Tortellini Soup

30 g (1 ounce) white sauce mix
3 boneless, skinless chicken
**   breast halves**
500 ml (14 ounces) chicken stock
1 teaspoon minced garlic
½ teaspoon dried basil
½ teaspoon oregano
½ teaspoon cayenne pepper
230 g (8 ounces) cheese
**   tortellini pasta**
1½ cups (465 g) unthickened
**   cream**
6 cups (180 g) fresh baby spinach

- Place white sauce mix in sprayed 5 to 6-L (5 to 6-quart) slow cooker.

- Stir in 4 cups (1 L) water and stir gradually until mixture is smooth.

- Cut chicken into 2.5-cm (1-inch) pieces. Add chicken, stock, garlic, basil, oregano, cayenne pepper and ½ teaspoon (2 ml) salt to mixture.

- Cover and cook on low for 6 to 7 hours or on high for 3 hours.

- Stir in pasta, cover and cook for additional 1 hour on high.

- Stir in cream and fresh spinach. Cook just enough for soup to get hot. Serves 4 to 6.

TIP: Sprinkle a little shredded parmesan cheese on top of each serving.

Beans and Pasta Soup

2 tablespoons (30 ml) olive oil
1 onion, chopped
2 sticks celery, sliced
2 teaspoons minced garlic
1 425-g (15-ounce) can
   borlotti beans
1 425-g (15-ounce) can
   kidney beans, rinsed, drained
1 230-g (8-ounce) can butter beans
1 cup (140 g) cooked,
   shredded ham
2 litres (56 ounces) chicken stock
2 bay leaves
1 cup (105 g) rigatoni (large
   tubes) pasta

- Heat oil in large soup pot and cook onion, celery and garlic on medium heat for about 5 minutes.

- Stir in borlotti beans, kidney beans, butter beans, ham, stock and bay leaves. Bring to a boil, reduce heat and simmer for about 30 minutes.

- Bring bean mixture back to boiling, add pasta, reduce heat to medium, cover and cook for about 12 to 14 minutes or until pasta is tender. Remove bay leaves before serving. Serves 8.

Pasta made from spelt can sometimes be tolerated by those allergic to gluten. Spelt is a different variety of wheat with a lower gluten content than common wheat, and has been cultivated for at least 4,000 years.

Ham, Bean and Pasta Soup

1 onion, finely chopped
2 sticks celery, chopped
2 teaspoons minced garlic
1 litre (28 ounces) chicken stock
420 g (15 ounces) can baked beans
    in ham sauce
3 cups (420 g) cooked, cubed ham
⅓ cup (35 g) macaroni (tube) pasta
Bacon cooked crisp, crumbled

- Combine onion, celery, garlic, chicken stock, beans, ham and 1 cup (250 ml) water in 5 to 6-L (5 to 6-quart) slow cooker.

- Cover and cook on low for 4 to 5 hours.

- Turn cooker to high heat, add pasta and cook for additional 35 to 45 minutes or until pasta is tender.

- Garnish each serving with cooked, crisp and crumbled bacon. Serves 6 to 8.

Italian Vegetable Soup

455 g (1 pound) bulk Italian
    sausages, sliced
2 onions, chopped
2 teaspoons minced garlic
30 g (1 ounce) beef-flavoured
    soup mix
1 425-g (15-ounce) can sliced
    carrots, drained
2 425-g (15-ounce) cans Italian
    stewed tomatoes
2 425-g (15-ounce) cans
    chickpeas, drained
1 cup (105 g) elbow macaroni
    (tube) pasta

- Brown sausages, onions and garlic in large soup pot. Pour off fat and add 4 cups (1 L) water, soup mix, carrots, tomatoes and chickpeas. Bring to a boil, reduce heat to low and simmer for 25 minutes.

- Add pasta and continue cooking for additional 15 to 20 minutes or until pasta is tender. Serves 8.

Sausage-Tortellini Soup

455 g (1 pound) Italian sausages,
    sliced
1 onion, chopped
3 sticks celery, sliced
1 litre (28 ounces) beef stock
½ teaspoon dried basil
1 425-g (15-ounce) can
    sliced carrots, drained
1 medium zucchini,
    halved, sliced
1 280-g (10-ounce) can Italian
    stewed tomatoes
255 g (9 ounces) refrigerated
    meat-filled tortellini pasta
Mozzarella cheese

- Cook and stir sausage, onion and celery in soup pot on medium heat until sausage is light brown.

- Drain and stir in beef stock, 1½ cups (375 ml) water, basil, carrots, zucchini, tomatoes, pasta and a little salt and pepper.

- Boil, reduce heat and simmer for 20 minutes or until pasta is tender.

- Ladle into individual soup bowls and sprinkle each serving with cheese. Serves 4 to 6.

The first known written recipe for pasta dates to about the year 1000 in a cookbook written in Sicily.

Mama Mia Chicken Chowder

3–4 (750 g) cooked boneless chicken
   breasts, shredded
¼ cup (60 ml) Italian salad
   dressing
1 425-g (15-ounce) can
   stewed tomatoes
1¾ cups (400 ml) chicken stock
2 small zucchini, chopped
½ cup (55 g) elbow macaroni
   (tube) pasta
1 teaspoon dried basil
1 cup (115 g) shredded
   mozzarella cheese

- Combine chicken, salad dressing, tomatoes, stock, zucchini, pasta, basil, ½ cup (125 ml) water and a little salt and pepper in large soup pot.

- Boil, reduce heat and simmer for 10 minutes or until pasta is tender. Serve in individual soup bowls and sprinkle cheese over each serving. Serves 6.

Vegetarian Chilli

2 425-g (15-ounce) cans
   stewed tomatoes
1 425-g (15-ounce) can kidney
   beans, rinsed, drained
1 425-g (15-ounce) can borlotti
   beans with liquid
1 onion, chopped
1 green capsicum,
   seeded, chopped
1 tablespoon (15 ml) paprika
340 g (12 ounces) elbow macaroni
   (tube) pasta
¼ cup (60 g) butter, sliced

- Combine tomatoes, kidney beans, borlotti beans, onion, capsicum, paprika and 1 cup (250 ml) water in soup pot. Cover and cook on medium heat for 1 hour.

- Cook pasta in saucepan according to package directions, drain and add butter. Stir until butter melts. Add pasta to chilli and mix well. Serves 6.

Turkey-Veggie Chilli

455 g (1 pound) minced turkey
Olive oil
2 425-g (15-ounce) cans borlotti
    beans with liquid
1 425-g (15-ounce) can
    cannellini beans with liquid
½ litre (14 ounces) chicken stock
2 425-g (15-ounce) cans
    stewed tomatoes
1 230-g (8-ounce) can
    corn kernels
1 large onion, chopped
1 red capsicum, seeded, chopped
2 teaspoons minced garlic
2 teaspoons ground cumin
2 teaspoons paprika
½ cup (55 g) elbow macaroni
    (tube) pasta

- Cook and brown turkey in frypan with a little oil before placing in large slow cooker.

- Add beans, stock, tomatoes, corn, onion, capsicum, garlic, cumin, paprika and a little salt and stir well.

- Cover and cook on low for 4 to 5 hours.

- Stir in pasta and continue cooking for about 15 minutes. Stir to make sure pasta does not stick to cooker and cook for additional 15 minutes or until it is tender. Serves 6 to 8.

TIP: *Top each serving with dab of sour cream or 1 tablespoon (15 ml) shredded cheddar cheese.*

Italian-Vegetable Stew

680–910 g (1½–2 pounds) Italian sausages sliced
910 g (32 ounces) frozen vegetables
2 425-g (15-ounce) cans Italian stewed tomatoes
½ litre (14 ounces) beef stock
1 teaspoon Italian seasoning
½ cup (50 g) gnocchi

- Brown sausage in frypan and cook for about 5 minutes and drain.

- Combine sausage, vegetables, stewed tomatoes, stock, Italian seasoning and pasta in 5 to 6-L (5 to 6-quart) slow cooker and mix well.

- Cover and cook on low for 3 to 5 hours. Serves 4 to 6.

Chicken-Tortellini Stew

255 g (9 ounces) cheese-filled tortellini pasta
2 medium yellow squash, halved, sliced
1 red capsicum, seeded, coarsely chopped
1 onion, chopped
1 litre (28 ounces) chicken stock
1 teaspoon dried rosemary
½ teaspoon dried basil
2 cups (280 g) cooked, chopped chicken

- Place pasta, squash, capsicum and onion in slow cooker. Stir in stock, rosemary, basil and chicken.

- Cover and cook on low for 2 to 4 hours or until pasta and vegetables are tender. Serves 4.

Scrumptious
Salads

*Veggie salads and meat salads
that can be a complete meal
are filling, tasty and easy.*

Scrumptious Salads Contents

A Unique
Salad Blend

170 g (6 ounces) Asian ramen
noodles, crushed
1 cup (170 g) slivered almonds,
toasted
¼ cup (30 g) sunflower kernels
¼ cup (60 g) butter, melted
1 head Chinese cabbage,
finely shredded
1 red capsicum, seeded,
finely chopped
1 bunch spring onions, sliced
¾ cup (175 ml) olive oil
¼ cup (60 ml) white vinegar
½ cup (100 g) sugar
2 tablespoons (30 ml) light soy
sauce

- Brown noodles, almonds and sunflower kernels with melted butter in large frypan over low heat. Remove from heat and cool.

- For dressing, combine olive oil, vinegar and sugar in small saucepan on high heat. Boil for 1 minute and add soy sauce.

- Combine noodle-almond mixture, Chinese cabbage, capsicum and spring onions in large bowl. Drizzle dressing over salad and toss to coat well. Serves 8 to 10.

Broccoli-Noodle Crunch Salad

*Who thought up the idea of grating
broccoli 'stems' for a salad? It
was pure genius! This salad is
different – and very good. It
will last and stay crisp in
the refrigerator for days!*

**1 cup (170 g) slivered almonds,
  toasted
1 cup (130 g) sunflower seeds,
  toasted
2 85-g (3-ounce) chicken-flavoured
  ramen noodles
1 cup (110 g) shredded broccli stems
1 cup (110 g) shredded carrot
1 cup (110 g) shredded red cabbage
¾ cup (175 ml) olive oil
½ cup (125 ml) white vinegar
½ cup (100 g) sugar
Ramen noodles seasoning
  packets**

- Preheat oven to 135° C (275° F).

- Toast almonds and sunflower seeds
  in oven for 15 minutes. Break up
  ramen noodles (but do not cook)
  and mix with broccoli, carrot,
  cabbage, almonds and sunflower
  seeds.

- In separate bowl, combine
  olive oil, vinegar, sugar and noodle
  seasoning packet. Pour over salad
  and mix well. Prepare at least
  1 hour before serving.
  Serves 10 to 12.

*TIP: Add a handful of broccoli
        florets just to make it prettier!*

Colour-Coded Salad

455 g (16 ounces) tri-coloured fusilli
    (spiral) pasta, cooked, drained
1 red capsicum, julienned
1 cup (125 g) chopped zucchini
1 cup (70 g) broccoli florets
1 cup (250 ml) Caesar salad dressing
1 green capsicum, julienned
⅔ cup (70 g) grated parmesan cheese

- Combine all ingredients except dressing in bowl.

- Toss with dressing. Refrigerate. Serves 4.

Colourful Garden Salad

230 g (8 ounces) multi-colour
    tortellini pasta
1 tablespoon olive oil
1 230-g (8-ounce) can cut green
    beans, drained
1 cup (130 g) diced carrots
1 cup (150 g) cherry tomato halves
1 yellow capsicum, seeded, julienned
230 g (8 ounces) cubed
    cheddar cheese
1 230-g (8-ounce) bottle
    Italian dressing

- Cook pasta in saucepan according to package directions, drain and rinse in cold water. Transfer to bowl and drizzle a little oil over pasta. Add green beans, carrots, tomatoes, capsicum and cheese and toss.

- Pour dressing over salad and toss to make sure dressing coats all ingredients. Cover and refrigerate for several hours before serving. Serves 8.

Fusilli Pasta Salad

455 g (16 ounces) fusilli (spiral) pasta
455 g (16 ounces) frozen broccoli-cauliflower combination
230 g (8 ounces) cubed mozzarella cheese
1 230-g (8-ounce) bottle of Italian salad dressing

- Cook pasta in saucepan according to package directions. Drain and cool.

- Cook vegetables according to package directions. Drain and cool.

- Combine pasta, vegetables and cheese chunks in large bowl.

- Toss with Italian dressing. Refrigerate several hours before serving. Serves 6.

Vegetable Salad

455 g (16 ounces) tri-coloured tube pasta
1 red capsicum, seeded, julienned
1 cup (150 g) cherry tomato halves
2 cups (140 g) small broccoli florets
1 cup (250 ml) refrigerated Caesar salad dressing

- Cook pasta in saucepan according to package directions and drain. Place in container with lid and add capsicum, tomatoes, broccoli and a little salt and pepper.

- Toss with salad dressing. Use more if needed to coat salad well. Cover and refrigerate for several hours before serving. Serves 6 to 8.

Fusilli pasta gets its name from the Italian for 'rifle' because its shape resembles the device inside the barrel of a firearm.

Harvest Pasta Salad

255 g (9 ounces) refrigerated
    cheese-stuffed tortellini pasta
1 455-g (16-ounce) bottle
    Italian salad dressing
2 cups (140 g) fresh broccoli florets
2 cups (200 g) fresh cauliflower
    florets
2 cups (300 g) cherry tomato
    halves
1 yellow capsicum, seeded,
    julienned
1 115-g (4-ounce) can black olives,
    drained
½ cup (50 g) grated parmesan
    cheese
⅓ cup (40 g) toasted sunflower
    seeds

- Cook pasta in saucepan according to package directions; drain, rinse in cold water and drain again. Place in bowl with lid and pour about ½ cup (125 ml) salad dressing over pasta and toss.

- Add broccoli, cauliflower, tomatoes, capsicum, olives and cheese to pasta. Add another ½ cup (125 ml) dressing and toss. Keep adding a little more dressing until vegetables and pasta are coated well.

- Cover and refrigerate for 2 to 3 hours before serving. Sprinkle sunflower seeds over top of salad before serving. Serves 10.

Nutty Pasta Slaw

230 g (8 ounces) fettuccini
    (medium egg noodles) pasta
½ cup (125 ml) peanut sauce
½ cup (125 ml) vegetable stock
1 tablespoon (15 ml) finely chopped,
    peeled fresh ginger
1 tablespoon (15 ml) olive oil
1 cup (220 g) shredded broccoli
    stems
1 cup (110 g) shredded red cabbage
2 cups (110 g) shredded carrots
2 tablespoons (30 ml) olive oil

- Cook pasta in saucepan according to package directions, drain and return to pot. Using kitchen scissors, snip pasta into small pieces. Cover and keep warm.

- Whisk peanut sauce and vegetable stock in small bowl and set aside. Stir-fry ginger in hot oil in large frypan on medium heat for just 15 seconds.

- Add broccoli, cabbage, carrots and olive oil, cook and stir for 1 minute. Stir in peanut-stock mixture to coat vegetables well and cook for additional 2 minutes.

- Add pasta and use tongs to toss mixture well. Serve warm. Serves 4 to 6.

Most pasta recipes are designed for using dried pastas.
Fresh pastas cook faster than dried pasta but are best used
with lighter sauces with cream or cheese. Dried pastas
work better with heavier sauces, casseroles and salads.

Pasta-Veggie Salad

455 g (16 ounces) cavatappi
  (corkscrew) pasta
455 g (16 ounces) frozen broccoli-
  cauliflower mixture,
  thawed
230 g (8 ounces) mozzarella cheese,
  cubed
1 230-g (8-ounce) bottle Italian
  salad dressing

• Cook pasta in saucepan according
  to package directions, drain and
  cool. Cook vegetables according to
  package directions, drain and cool.

• Combine pasta, vegetables and
  cheese in large bowl and toss
  with salad dressing. Refrigerate
  for several hours before serving.
  Serves 10.

Pasta Plus

455 g (16 ounces) rainbow
  rotini (spiral) pasta
2 cups (140 g) small fresh broccoli
  florets
2 cups (200 g) small cauliflower
  florets
1 cup (135 g) baby carrots, halved
  lengthwise
1 red capsicum, seeded, julienned
1 packet French onion soup mix
2 cups (16 ounces) water

• Cook pasta in saucepan according
  to package directions; drain and
  rinse in cold water.

• Place pasta in large salad bowl and
  add broccoli, cauliflower, carrots
  and capsicum.

• Add water to soup mix.

• Pour about three-fourths of the
  French onion 'soup' over salad, add
  more if needed and toss. Cover and
  refrigerate for 2 to 3 hours.
  Serves 8.

Pasta Plus Salad

**455 g (16 ounces) farfalle
   (bow-tie) pasta**
**280 g (10 ounces) frozen
   green peas, thawed**
**1 red capsicum, seeded,
   cut in strips**
**230 g (8 ounces) cubed
   Swiss cheese**
1 small yellow squash, sliced
¾ cup (170 g) mayonnaise
2 tablespoons (30 ml) lemon juice
1 tablespoon (15 ml) sugar
½ cup (40 g) pouring cream

- Cook pasta in saucepan according to package directions and add peas last 2 minutes of cooking time. Drain pasta and peas, rinse in cold water and drain again. Transfer to large salad bowl and add cheese, capsicum and squash.

- For dressing combine mayonnaise, lemon juice, sugar and pouring cream into a bowl and mix well. Spoon over salad with a little salt and pepper. Toss salad and refrigerate for several hours before serving. Serves 8.

Quinoa is a substitute for pasta for people with wheat allergies. Quinoa [keen WAH] is a grain from South America that has been in use for 6,000 years.

Pasta-Packed Dinner Salad

230 g (8 ounces) wholemeal penne (tube) pasta
1½ cups (425 g) black beans, soaked overnight
1½ cups (210 g) cooked, chopped chicken
1 small red capsicum, seeded, julienned
½ red onion, cut into thin wedges
2 cups (70 g) lightly packed rocket leaves, torn
2 tablespoons (2 g) snipped fresh coriander
½ cup (125 ml) orange juice
230 g (8 ounces) light sour cream
½ teaspoon lemon pepper
1 teaspoon ground mixed herbs

- Cook pasta in saucepan according to package directions; drain and rinse in cold water and drain again. Place pasta in large salad bowl and add black beans, chicken, capsicum and red onion; set aside.

- Combine orange juice, sour cream, lemon pepper and mixed herbs in small bowl. Spoon over salad mixture and toss to coat well. Cover and refrigerate for 3 hours or overnight.

- When ready to serve, mix in 1 tablespoon (15 ml) orange juice if needed for desired consistency. Add rocket and coriander and toss well. Serves 6.

Perfect Pasta Salad

230 g (8 ounces) cavatappi (corkscrew) pasta
2 cups (140 g) fresh broccoli florets
1 230-g (8-ounce) can sliced carrots, drained
½ cup (75 g) chopped red capsicum
½ cup (80 g) chopped red onion
¾ cup (170 g) mayonnaise
2 tablespoons (30 ml) white wine vinegar
1 tablespoon (15 ml) Dijon-style mustard
1 teaspoon sugar
1 teaspoon minced garlic

- Cook pasta in large saucepan according to package directions. Add broccoli to pasta cooking water during last 2 minutes. Drain pasta and broccoli and rinse with cold water to cool quickly.

- Combine mayonnaise, vinegar, mustard, sugar, garlic and a little salt and pepper in large bowl. Add pasta, broccoli, carrots, capsicum and onion and toss to coat well. Cover and refrigerate. Serves 8.

In the 17th century, a pasta machine was invented in Naples. This technological advance revolutionised production and made pasta less expensive.

Protein Plus Pasta Salad

230 g (8 ounces)
    macaroni (tube) pasta
1 425-g (15-ounce) can kidney
    beans, rinsed, drained
280 g (10 ounces) frozen green peas,
    thawed, drained
1 cup (70 g) shredded carrot
230 g (8 ounces) cubed
    cheddar cheese
1 red capsicum, seeded,
    chopped
¾ cup (170 g) mayonnaise
2 tablespoons (30 ml) olive oil
¼ cup (15 g) fresh chopped parsley
1 teaspoon minced garlic
1 teaspoon lemon pepper

- Cook pasta in saucepan according to package directions, drain and rinse in cold water. Transfer macaroni to large bowl.

- Place beans, peas, carrots, cheese and capsicum in bowl with macaroni.

- For dressing combine mayonnaise, olive oil, parsley, garlic and lemon pepper into a bowl.

- Stir in dressing and toss. Make sure dressing coats all ingredients. Add a little more oil if salad needs to be creamier. Refrigerate for 2 to 3 hours before serving. Serves 8.

15-Minute Pasta-Chicken Salad

340 g (12 ounces) conchiglie
  (small shells) pasta
280 g (10 ounces) frozen baby green
  peas, thawed
2 cups (12 ounces) shredded chicken
  breast, cooked
1 115-g (4-ounce) can sliced black
  olives
2 sticks celery, chopped
4 fresh spring onions, sliced
1 cup (225 g) mayonnaise

- Cook pasta in large pot of salted
  water according to package
  directions; drain and rinse in
  cold water.

- Combine pasta, peas, chicken,
  olives, celery, spring onions and a
  little salt and pepper in large bowl.
  Add mayonnaise and toss to mix
  well. If salad seems too dry, add a
  little more mayonnaise. Refrigerate
  until time to serve. Serves 8.

Sesame-Broccoli Salad

1½ cups (165 g) shredded broccoli
  stems
1½ cups (165 g) shredded carrot
1½ cups (165 g) shredded red
  cabbage
1 red capsicum, seeded,
  chopped
2 255-g (9-ounce) packets
  refrigerated tortellini pasta,
  cooked
1 230-g (8-ounce) bottle
  vinaigrette salad dressing
2 tablespoons (30 ml) olive oil
¼ cup (30 g) sesame seeds, toasted

- Combine broccoli, carrot, cabbage,
  capsicum and cooked pasta in
  salad bowl. Drizzle salad dressing
  and olive oil over salad and toss.
  Refrigerate. Just before serving,
  sprinkle sesame seeds over salad.
  Serves 8.

TIP: *Toasting brings out the flavours
      of nuts and seeds. Place nuts or
      seeds on baking tray and bake
      at 110° C (225° F) for
      10 minutes. Be careful not to
      burn them.*

Pool Party Pasta Salad

½ cup (65 g) pine nuts, toasted
1 230-g (8-ounce) bunch trimmed
    asparagus
455 g (16 ounces) farfalle
    (bow-tie) pasta
340 g (¾ pound) deli turkey, cut
    in 5-cm (2-inch) strips
1 red capsicum, seeded, chopped
1 400-g (14-ounce) can artichoke
    hearts, drained, sliced
3 fresh spring onions, sliced
1 230-g (8-ounce) bottle creamy
    salad dressing

- Toast pine nuts in small frypan over low heat for about 5 minutes or until golden. Set aside.

- Cut asparagus into 2.5-cm (1-inch) pieces. Cook pasta in saucepan according to package directions but add asparagus last minute of cooking time. Drain thoroughly and transfer to large baking tray to cool.

- Place all salad ingredients, except pine nuts, in large bowl and refrigerate for at least 1 hour. When ready to serve, add dressing and pine nuts and toss well to coat all ingredients. Serves 8 to 10.

Pasta is one of the most versatile dishes we know. It is very quick and simple to prepare and it easily takes on the flavours of sauces and seasonings.

Ready-To-Go Pasta Salad

1 455-g (16-ounce) package rotini
   (spiral) pasta
12 cherry tomatoes, halved, drained
4 fresh spring onions, sliced
1 115-g (4-ounce) can sliced black
   olives
¾ cup (110 g) chopped green
   capsicum
¾ cup (100 g) sliced salami,
   halved
1 230-g (8-ounce) package
   mozzarella cheese, cubed
½ cup (125 ml) olive oil
½ cup (125 ml) red wine vinegar
1 tablespoon (15 ml) sugar
1 teaspoon minced garlic
2 teaspoons dried basil

- Cook pasta in saucepan according
  to package directions and drain.
  Rinse in cold water and drain again.

- Combine pasta, tomatoes, spring
  onions, olives, capsicum, salami
  and cheese in large bowl and gently
  mix.

- For dressing whisk oil, vinegar,
  sugar, garlic, basil and a little
  salt and pepper in bowl. Drizzle
  dressing over salad and gently toss.

- Cover and refrigerate for at least
  2 hours or overnight. Serves 6 to 8.

*Pasta became popular very quickly from an early date not only because
it is delicious and nutritious, but because it has a long shelf life.*

Special Pasta Salad

1 455-g (16-ounce) tub prepared
    pasta salad
1 230-g (8-ounce) can corn kernels,
    drained
2 small zucchini, diced
⅔ cup (175 g) chunky salsa

- Combine pasta salad, corn, zucchini and salsa in salad bowl with lid and mix well. Cover and refrigerate until ready to serve. Serves 6.

Terrific Tortellini Salad

800 g (28 ounces) refrigerated cheese
    tortellini pasta
1 green capsicum, seeded, diced
1 red capsicum, seeded, diced
1 cucumber, chopped
1 400-g (14-ounce) can artichoke
    hearts, rinsed, drained
1 230-g (8-ounce) bottle creamy
    Caesar salad dressing

- Prepare pasta in saucepan according to package directions and drain.

- Rinse with cold water, drain and refrigerate.

- Combine pasta, capsicums, cucumber, artichoke hearts and dressing in large bowl. (You may want to add a little black pepper.)

- Cover and refrigerate for at least 2 hours before serving. Serves 6.

Summer Picnic Salad

230 g (8 ounces) cavatelli
  (shell) pasta
1 cup (115 g) shredded cheddar
  cheese
2 cups (140 g) fresh broccoli florets
½ cup (70 g) chopped salami
8 cherry tomatoes, halved
¼ cup (30 g) shredded mozzarella
  cheese
½ cup (125 ml) olive oil
3 tablespoons (45 ml) red wine
  vinegar
1 teaspoon dried basil
2 teaspoons sugar
Crushed dried chilli flakes

- Cook pasta in large saucepan according to package directions, drain and rinse under cold water. Place in bowl.

- For dressing combine olive oil, vinegar, basil, sugar and chilli flakes into a small bowl and stir until they blend well.

- Pour over pasta and toss; stir in cheddar cheese and toss again. Cover and refrigerate for 2 to 3 hours.

- Add broccoli, salami and tomato halves and toss well. Transfer to serving bowl and sprinkle mozzarella cheese over top. Serves 6.

If you do not use enough water when boiling pasta, the pasta will not cook evenly.

Tailgate Tortellini Salad

510 g (18 ounces) refrigerated
    meat-filled tortellini pasta
1 red capsicum, seeded, cubed
1 seedless cucumber, peeled, cubed
230 g (8 ounces) cubed
    mozzarella cheese
1 115-g (4-ounce) can sliced
    black olives, drained
1 teaspoon dried basil
¼ cup (60 ml) olive oil
2 tablespoons (30 ml) white wine
    vinegar
1 tablespoon (15 ml) balsamic
    vinegar
1 tablespoon (15 ml) sugar
Shredded lettuce

- Cook pasta in saucepan according to package directions and drain immediately. Rinse with cold water and drain again. Place pasta in large bowl and add capsicum, cucumber, mozzarella cheese, olives and a little salt and pepper.

- Combine basil, olive oil, white wine vinegar, balsamic vinegar and sugar in screw-top jar. Cover and shake well.

- Pour dressing over pasta mixture and gently toss to coat all ingredients. Serve on bed of shredded lettuce. Serves 6.

Tri-Colour Pasta Salad

3 cups (315 g) tri-colour fusilli
    (spiral) pasta
1 tablespoon (15 ml) olive oil
1 large bunch broccoli, cut
    into small florets
1 cup (100 g) chopped celery
1 cup (120 g) peeled, thinly sliced
    cucumber
455 g (1 pound) Swiss cheese,
    cubed
1 230-g (8-ounce) bottle creamy
    salad dressing

- Cook pasta in saucepan according
  to package directions and drain.
  Stir in olive oil and transfer to large
  salad bowl. Add broccoli florets,
  celery, cucumber, cheese and a
  little salt and pepper.

- Pour dressing over salad and toss.
  Refrigerate for several hours for
  flavours to blend. Serves 10.

Chicken or Turkey Salad

3 cups (420 g) cooked, chopped
    chicken or turkey
1 cup (100 g) celery
1½ cups (225 g) green grapes,
    halved
¾ cup (100 g) cashew nuts
¾ cup (170 g) mayonnaise
1 cup (55 g) thin crispy noodles
Cabbage leaves

- Combine chopped chicken, celery,
  grapes and cashew nuts in bowl and
  toss with mayonnaise. Just before
  serving, mix in noodles and serve
  on cabbage leaves. Serves 6.

Fruity Summer Macaroni Salad

340 g (12 ounces) elbow macaroni
  (tube) pasta
½ cup (85 g) slivered almonds,
  toasted
2 sticks celery, chopped
1 red capsicum, seeded, chopped
1 red apple with peel, diced
1 green apple with peel, diced
1 mandarin deseeded and segmented
1 cup (250 g) pineapple pieces,
  drained
1 tablespoon (15 ml) chopped
  fresh chives
1 cup (225 g) mayonnaise
1 tablespoon (15 ml) lemon juice
1 tablespoon (15 ml) sugar

- Cook pasta in saucepan according to package directions; drain and rinse in cold water. Set aside. Toast almonds for 10 minutes at 160° C (325° F).

- Combine celery, capsicum, apples, mandarin, pineapple, chives and a little salt and pepper in large bowl.

- For dressing combine mayonnaise, lemon juice and sugar into a bowl.

- Add pasta and almonds to celery-mandarin mixture and toss with dressing mixture to blend well. If salad seems too dry, add another tablespoon or 2 mayonnaise and toss. Cover and refrigerate until ready to serve. Serves 8.

The word macaroni (maccheroni in Italian) is thought to come from a Sicilian word 'maccarruni' which means made into a dough by force.

Chicken Salad Meal

340 g (12 ounces) farfalle or tripolini (bow-tie) pasta

2 425-g (15-ounce) cans three-bean mix with liquid, chilled

2½ cups (350 g) bite-size chunks roast chicken

1 cup (150 g) cherry tomatoes, halved

2 sticks celery, chopped

½ cup (125 ml) from bean mix juice

¼ cup (60 ml) olive oil

1 tablespoon (15 ml) Dijon-style mustard

¼ cup (60 g) mayonnaise

1 tablespoon (15 ml) sugar

1 teaspoon dried dill

- Cook pasta in saucepan according to package directions with 1 teaspoon salt; drain and rinse under cold water. Shake any excess water off pasta and place in large bowl.

- Drain juice from three-bean mix and set aside. Add three-bean mix, chicken, tomatoes and celery; stir well to combine; transfer to salad bowl.

- Place juice, olive oil, mustard, mayonnasie, sugar and dill into a jar and shake well to blend. Drizzle about half dressing over salad and toss gently to mix well. Refrigerate for about 20 minutes.

- When ready to serve, add more dressing as needed and toss again. Serves 8.

Chicken Pasta Joy

340 g (12 ounce) ziti (thin tubes)
    pasta
2 sticks celery, sliced
1 roasted red capsicum, chopped
1 red capsicum, seeded,
    cut into 2.5-cm (1-inch) strips
1 onion, chopped
6 boneless, skinless chicken
    breast halves, cooked
1 cup (140 g) cashew halves
1¼ cups (280 g) mayonnaise
⅓ cup (75 g) packed brown sugar
1 tablespoon (15 ml) lemon juice
1 tablespoon (15 ml) white vinegar

- Cook pasta in saucepan according to package directions; drain and rinse under cold water. Transfer to large bowl. Cut chicken into bite-size pieces. Add celery, roasted capsicum, capsicum, onion, chicken and a little salt and pepper. Toss to mix well.

- Combine mayonnaise, brown sugar, lemon juice, vinegar and a little salt in small bowl. Pour over salad, toss, cover and refrigerate until ready to serve. Stir in cashews just before serving. Serves 8.

The first pasta factory in Venice was licensed in 1740.

Chicken-Curry Salad

½ litre (14 ounces) chicken stock
2–3 boneless, skinless
    chicken breast halves
230 g (8 ounces) conchiglie
    (medium shells) pasta
1 115-g (4-ounce) can chopped
    black olives, drained
1 red capsicum, seeded, chopped
1 apple, peeled, cored, sliced
2 sticks celery, chopped
½ cup (120 g) sour cream
½ cup (115 g) mayonnaise
1 teaspoon minced garlic
¾ teaspoon curry powder

- Place chicken stock and chicken in large saucepan and cook on medium-high heat for about 12 to 14 minutes. Remove chicken and leave stock in saucepan. Cool chicken, cut into bite-size chunks and set aside.

- With remaining stock, add enough water to cook pasta according to package directions. Drain and rinse in cold water. Discard remaining stock.

- Combine sour cream, mayonnaise, garlic, curry powder and a little salt and pepper in small bowl. Combine cooled pasta, chicken, dressing, olives, capsicum, apple and celery in large bowl.

- Mix well and refrigerate for at least 3 hours before serving. Serves 4 to 6.

Colourful Salad that Packs a Punch

230 g (8 ounces) cavatappi
   (corkscrew) pasta
2½ cups (600 ml) bite-size pieces
   roast chicken without skin
½ cup (120 ml) grated carrot
2 sticks celery, chopped
1 red capsicum, seeded, chopped
1 bunch fresh spring onions, sliced
1 cos lettuce torn
250 ml (8 ounces) blue cheese
   dressing
½ cup (120 g) sour cream
¼ cup (70 g) bottled chilli sauce
1 tablespoon (15 ml) barbecue
   sauce
2 teaspoons paprika
⅓ teaspoon cayenne pepper

- Cook pasta in saucepan according to package directions; drain and rinse in cold water.

- Place in large bowl. Add chicken, carrots, celery, capsicum and onions. Refrigerate for about 20 minutes.

- For dressing, combine blue cheese dressing, sour cream, chilli sauce, barbecue sauce, paprika and cayenne pepper plus 1 teaspoon salt in bowl and mix well. Dressing can be made ahead of time.

- Pour dressing over salad and toss to coat well. Line serving platter with lettuce and spoon salad on top. Serves 8.

Exciting Grilled Chicken Salad

6 boneless, skinless chicken
    breast halves
Cajun seasoning
340 g (12 ounces) rotini
    (short spirals) pasta
340 g (12 ounces) cubed mozzarella
    cheese
1 red onion, chopped
1 yellow capsicum, seeded, chopped
280 g (10 ounces) frozen
    baby green peas, thawed
1 head cos lettuce, torn
1–1½ cups (250–360 ml) refrigerated
    honey-mustard dressing

- Preheat grill to high heat. Season both sides of chicken breasts with ample amount of Cajun seasoning. Grill chicken for 6 to 8 minutes (according to size) on each side or until juices run clear.

- Remove from heat and place on plate to cool. When chicken is cool enough, cut into strips. Refrigerate.

- Cook pasta in saucepan according to package directions, drain and rinse in cold water; set aside.

- Mix cheese, onion, capsicum, peas and lettuce in large bowl. When chicken and pasta chill, add to cheese-lettuce mixture and toss.

- Pour in 1 cup (250 ml) honey-mustard dressing and toss again. Add more dressing, if needed. Refrigerate until time to serve. Serves 6 to 8.

Mandarin Chicken Salad

2 tablespoons (30 g) butter
85 g (3 ounces) Oriental-flavoured
    ramen noodle soup mix
3 cups (420 g) cooked, cubed
    chicken
⅓ cup (50 g) dry-roasted peanuts
455 g (16 ounces) of coleslaw mix
1 310-g (11-ounce) can mandarin
    segments, drained
⅓ cup (70 g) sugar
⅓ cup (75 ml) white vinegar
¼ cup (60 ml) olive oil

- Melt butter in large frypan over medium heat. Stir in seasoning packet from soup mix. Break up block of noodles into bite-sized pieces and stir into butter mixture.

- Cook noodles for 3 to 4 minutes, stirring often, until noodles are golden brown. Remove from heat and place in large bowl. Stir in chicken, peanuts, coleslaw and mandarin segments and mix well.

- For dressing combine sugar, vinegar and olive oil into a small bowl and pour over salad and toss. Serves 8 to 10.

New Classic Caesar Pasta

455 g (16 ounces) penne
    (tube) pasta
2 tablespoons (30 g) butter
4 boneless, skinless chicken
    breast halves, cut in strips
230 g (8 ounces) cubed
    cheddar cheese
1 red capsicum, seeded, chopped
1 head cos lettuce, torn
1 large tomato, chopped, drained
250 ml (8 ounces) Caesar
    salad dressing
¼ cup (60 ml) red wine vinegar
1 tablespoon (15 ml) sugar

- Cook pasta in saucepan according to package directions and drain; transfer to large bowl.

- Melt butter in large frypan over medium-high heat and cook chicken for about 10 minutes or until juices run clear. Remove frypan from heat.

- For dressing combine Caesar dressing, vinegar and sugar into a jar and shake well.

- Add chicken, cheese, capsicum and lettuce to pasta and toss.

- Pour dressing over mixture and toss again. Garnish with chopped tomato and serve immediately. Serves 8.

Corn pasta works well for those allergic to wheat; however, it tends to have a 'mushy' consistency.

Chicken Mediterranean Salad

210 g (7.5 ounces) pre-made creamy
    pasta salad
3 tablespoons (45 ml) olive oil
1½ cups (210 g) cooked,
    cubed chicken
3 fresh spring onions, sliced
1 medium tomato, chopped,
    drained
1 200-g (7-ounce) jar basil pesto

- Combine olive oil and pasta salad
  in large bowl. Stir in chicken,
  onions, tomato and pesto. Serves 8.

Quick-Fix Salad

115 g (8 ounces) spaghetti pasta
1 cup (140 g) cooked, shredded
    chicken breast
½ cup (60 g) peeled, diced
    cucumber
½ cup (60 g) sliced baby carrots
½ cup (50 g) green peas
1 tablespoon (15 ml) white vinegar
1 tablespoon (15 ml) light soy sauce
1 tablespoon (15 ml) olive oil
1 teaspoon sugar
½ teaspoon minced garlic

- Cook pasta in saucepan according
  to package directions, drain and
  rinse in cold water. Drain again.

- Combine pasta, chicken, cucumber,
  carrots, peas and a little salt and
  pepper in bowl.

- Combine vinegar, soy sauce, oil,
  sugar and garlic in small saucepan.
  Bring to a boil, remove from heat
  and drizzle over spaghetti mixture.
  Toss to coat well. Serves 2 to 3.

Noodle-Turkey Salad

85 g (3 ounces) oriental-flavoured ramen noodle soup mix
455 g (16 ounces) finely shredded coleslaw mix
340 g (¾ pound) smoked turkey, cut into strips
½ cup (125 ml) vinaigrette salad dressing

- Coarsely crush noodles and place in bowl with lid. Add coleslaw mix and turkey strips.

- Combine vinaigrette salad dressing and seasoning packet from noodle mix in small bowl, pour over noodle-turkey mixture and toss to coat mixture well. Refrigerate before serving. Serves 4.

Pasta Salad Dinner

340 g (12 ounces) tri-colour fusilli (spiral) pasta
1 115-g (4-ounce) can sliced black olives, drained
2 cups (140 g) fresh broccoli florets, chopped
2 small yellow squash, sliced
230 g (8 ounces) creamy salad dressing
1.4 kg (3 pounds) smoked turkey breast, sliced

- Cook pasta in saucepan according to package directions, drain and rinse in cold water. Place in large salad bowl and add olives, broccoli and squash.

- Pour dressing over salad mixture and toss. Place turkey on top of salad. Serves 8.

TIP: You won't need all the turkey, but what's left will make great sandwiches!

Perky Party Pasta

**455 g (1 pound) minced turkey or
    minced chicken**
**¼ cup (30 g) seasoned
    breadcrumbs**
1 teaspoon minced garlic
1 large egg
**1 cup (100 g) grated romano
    cheese**
**455 g (16 ounces) farfalle (bow-tie)
    pasta**
1 tablespoon (15 ml) cornflour
1 cup (250 ml) milk
**½ litre (14 ounces) chicken
    stock**
255 g (9 ounces) baby spinach

- Preheat oven to 190° C (375° F).

- Combine minced turkey,
  breadcrumbs, garlic, egg and ¼ cup
  (60 ml) cheese in medium bowl.
  Mix just until they blend well and
  shape into 36 (2.5-cm/1-inch)
  meatballs.

- Place meatballs on foil-lined
  25 x 38-cm (10 x 15-inch) tray and
  bake for 20 minutes.

- Cook pasta in large saucepan
  according to package directions,
  drain and return to saucepan.

- Whisk cornflour into milk in
  2-cup (500-ml) measuring cup.
  Add stock and pour into saucepan
  with pasta. Bring mixture to
  boiling, stir often and cook for
  1 minute to thicken sauce slightly.

- Remove saucepan from heat
  and stir in spinach, ½ cup (50 g)
  cheese and meatballs. Gently toss
  to blend. Spoon into sprayed 3-L
  (3-quart) baking dish. Sprinkle with
  remaining cheese and bake for
  20 minutes. Serves 6.

Picnic Pasta Salad

230 g (8 ounces) maruzze (shell)
   pasta
1 cup (130 g) cubed cheddar cheese
2 sticks celery, sliced
1 red capsicum, seeded, chopped
280 g (10 ounces) frozen green peas,
   thawed
¼ cup (60 g) gherkin relish
½ cup (110 g) mayonnaise
⅔ cup (150 ml) creamy salad
   dressing

- Cook pasta in saucepan according
  to package directions, rinse under
  cold water and drain.

- Combine pasta, cheese, celery,
  capsicum, peas, relish and a little
  salt and pepper in bowl.

- Stir in mayonnaise and dressing
  and toss. Cover and refrigerate for
  at least 24 hours before serving.
  Serves 6.

Pasta-Turkey Salad Dinner

340 g (12 ounces) tri-colour fusilli
   (spiral) pasta
1 115-g (4-ounce) can sliced black
   olives, drained
1 cup (70 g/100 g) each fresh
   broccoli and cauliflower florets
2 small yellow squash, sliced
1 cup (150 g) halved cherry
   tomatoes
230 g (8 ounces) creamy salad
   dressing
680 g (1½ pounds) smoked
   turkey breast, sliced

- Cook pasta in saucepan according
  to package directions. Drain and
  rinse in cold water. Place in large
  salad bowl and add olives, broccoli,
  cauliflower, squash and tomatoes.

- Toss with dressing. Place thin slices
  of turkey breast, arranged in rows,
  over salad. Serve immediately.
  Serves 8.

Tuna-Veggie Salad

230 g (8 ounces) maruzze (shell)
    pasta
2 small yellow squash, chopped
2 small zucchini, chopped
1 425-g (15-ounce) can borlotti
    beans, rinsed, drained
1 310-g (11-ounce) can
    corn kernels, drained
1 340-g (12-ounce) can tuna,
    drained
1 cup (250 ml) creamy Italian
    salad dressing
½ green capsicum, finely diced
½ red capsicum, finely diced

- Cook pasta in saucepan according to package directions, drain and rinse in cold water.

- Place squash and zucchini in saucepan with about ¾ cup (175 ml) water and cook on medium-high heat for 10 minutes or just until they are barely tender. Drain well.

- Combine pasta, squash, zucchini, beans, capsicums, corn, tuna and a little salt and pepper in large bowl. Refrigerate for at least 1 hour. Add salad dressing and toss to mix well. Refrigerate. Serves 6 to 8.

What's the difference between pasta and noodles? Noodles are a form of pasta made of durum flour (more finely ground than semolina), water and eggs. Eggs are a required ingredient. All other forms of pasta are made from semolina flour and water.

Tuna-Tortellini Salad

200 g (7 ounces) spaghetti, broken
¼ cup (60 g) butter
1 340-g (12-ounce) can tuna,
    drained
1 115-g (4-ounce) can sliced
    black olives
¾ cup (55 g) pouring cream
1 teaspoon dried basil leaves
2 tablespoons (10 g) grated
    parmesan cheese

- Cook pasta in saucepan according to package directions, drain, add butter and stir until butter melts. Add tuna and olives.

- Combine dressing ingredients with 1 teaspoon salt in bowl. Pour over spaghetti-tuna mixture and toss. Serves 4.

Garden Crab Salad

340 g (12 ounces) tri-colour fusilli or
    rotini (spiral) pasta
1 head fresh broccoli, cut
    into small florets
1 small head cauliflower,
    cut into small florets
1 red capsicum, seeded, chopped
455 g (16 ounces) imitation
    crabmeat, flaked
230 g (8 ounces) vinaigrette
    salad dressing
2 tablespoons (15 g) dry roasted
    sunflower kernels

- Cook pasta in saucepan according to package directions; drain and rinse in cold water.

- Combine broccoli, cauliflower, capsicum and crabmeat in large bowl. Pour vinaigrette dressing over salad and toss. Sprinkle sunflower kernels over top.

- Refrigerate for at least 1 to 2 hours before serving. Serves 6 to 8.

Easy Macaroni-Tuna Salad

3 cups (315 g) elbow macaroni (tube) pasta
1 340-g (12-ounce) can tuna, drained, flaked
1 red onion, chopped
2 sticks celery, chopped
1 roasted red capsicum chopped
1 115-g (4-ounce) can chopped black olives
½ cup (125 ml) creamy Italian salad dressing
½ cup (120 g) sour cream
½ cup (110 g) mayonnaise
½ teaspoon garlic powder

- Cook pasta in saucepan according to package directions. (Macaroni can be cooked ahead of time.)

- Drain, rinse in cold water and drain again. Transfer to large bowl and add tuna, onion, celery, roasted red capsicum and olives; mix well.

- Combine Italian dressing, sour cream, mayonnaise, garlic powder, 1 teaspoon salt and ½ teaspoon black pepper in bowl.

- Stir into macaroni-tuna mixture and toss. Refrigerate for several hours before serving. Refrigerate any leftover salad. Serves 6.

Lemony Crab Salad

230 g (8 ounces) farfalle (bow-tie) pasta
1 seedless cucumber, peeled, sliced
1 stick celery, chopped
1 red capsicum, seeded, chopped
4 fresh spring onions, sliced
455 g (16 ounces) imitation crabmeat, flaked
1 lemon, sliced thinly
½ cup (120 g) sour cream
⅔ cup (150 g) mayonnaise
2 tablespoons (30 ml) lemon juice
1 teaspoon sugar
½ teaspoon dried dill

- Cook pasta in saucepan according to package directions; drain and rinse with cold water. Rinse again with cold water and set aside.

- Combine all dressing ingredients plus a little salt and pepper in large bowl; mix well.

- Add pasta, cucumber, celery, capsicum and onion and toss. Stir in crabmeat and gently toss again.

- Cover and refrigerate for at least 1 hour before serving. Garnish with lemon slices. Serves 6.

Linguine-Crab Reward

**455 g (16 ounces) linguine
(thin egg noodles) pasta
255 g (9 ounces) mixed
salad greens
455 g (16 ounces) imitation
crabmeat, flaked
1 roasted red capsicum, chopped
¼ cup (40 g) chopped gherkins
¾ cup (175 ml) light soy sauce
½ cup (125 ml) extra-virgin olive oil
½ cup (100 g) sugar
⅓ cup (75 ml) white vinegar
1 tablespoon (15 ml) sesame seeds**

- Cook pasta in saucepan according to package directions and drain.

- Combine all dressing ingredients in jar with lid and shake to mix well. Refrigerate.

- Toss pasta, salad greens, crabmeat, roasted red capsicum, gherkins and a little salt and pepper in large bowl.

- For dressing combine soy sauce, olive oil, sugar, vinegar and sesame seeds into a bowl. Pour about half dressing over salad, toss and add more dressing as needed. Refrigerate until serving.
Serves 8 to 10.

Pasta nera *or black pasta is sometimes known as squid-ink pasta because it is flavoured with squid 'ink'. This gives it its distinctive black colour. It is usually served with shellfish.*

Angel Prawn Supreme

455 g (16 ounces) capelli d'angelo
   (angel hair) pasta
455 g (16 ounces) frozen prawn
   meat, thawed, drained
1 bunch fresh spring onions
   with tops, chopped
1 red capsicum, seeded,
   finely chopped
2 sticks celery, sliced
455 g (16 ounces) creamy salad
   dressing

- Break strands of pasta in half; then cook in saucepan according to package directions, drain and rinse under cold water. Place in large bowl.

- Stir in prawn meat, onions, capsicum and celery and toss. Add 1½ cups (375 ml) salad dressing and toss again. Refrigerate for at least 2 hours before serving.

- After salad stands, you may want to add a little more dressing before serving. Serves 6 to 8.

Water should be at a full rolling boil before adding pasta. When the water returns to a boil, the heat may be lowered so it continues to cook at a low boil. Unlike rice, pasta should not be covered when cooking and should be stirred now and then to keep the pieces from sticking to each other.

Seafood Medley Salad

455 g (16 ounces) shell pasta
1 170-g (6-ounce) can crabmeat, drained
1 170-g (6-ounce) can tuna, drained
1 170-g (6-ounce) can prawn meat, drained
½ cup (80 g) gherkins, chopped
2 sticks celery, sliced
2 carrots, grated
1 cup (225 g) mayonnaise
⅓ cup (75 ml) French salad dressing
¼ cup (60 ml) milk
1 tablespoon (15 ml) lemon juice
1 tablespoon (15 ml) sugar

- Cook shell pasta in saucepan according to package directions. Drain and rinse with cold water. Combine crabmeat, tuna, prawn meat, gherkins, celery and carrots in large bowl.

- For dressing combine mayonnaise, salad dressing, milk, lemon juice and sugar into a small bowl and mix well. Add pasta to seafood mixture, spoon on dressing and toss well. Cover and refrigerate until cold or overnight. Serves 8 to 10.

Superb Seafood Salad

455 g (16 ounces) tube pasta
3 eggs, hard-boiled, chopped
280 g (10 ounces) frozen baby green
    peas, thawed
1 red capsicum, seeded,
    finely chopped
2 sticks celery, chopped
230 g (8 ounces) frozen, thawed
    prawn meat, shredded
455 g (16 ounces) imitation
    crabmeat, flaked
Paprika
455 g (1 pint) mayonnaise
1 tablespoon (15 ml) lemon juice
2 teaspoons (10 ml) sugar
1 teaspoon dried parsley
1 teaspoon Cajun seasoning

- Cook pasta in saucepan according to package directions, drain and rinse with cold water. Transfer to large bowl and add eggs, peas, capsicum, celery, prawn meat and crabmeat. Cover and refrigerate.

- For dressing combine mayonnaise, lemon juice, sugar, parsley and seasoning into a bowl and mix well. Spoon over salad ingredients and toss until they mix well.

- If salad seems a little dry, stir in 1 tablespoon (15 ml) milk. Refrigerate for at least 1 to 2 hours before serving. Garnish with sprinkles of paprika. Serves 10 to 12.

Pasta
with Beef

*Appetising and hearty recipes
with beef at the centre
make pasta a family favourite.*

Pasta with Beef Contents

Bold Chilli over Pasta

1 kg (2 pounds) lean minced beef
1 onion, chopped
2 teaspoons minced garlic
1 425-g (15-ounce) can stewed
   tomatoes
1 teaspoon paprika
1 green chilli, chopped
1 425-g (15-ounce) can borlotti
   beans, drained
1 230-g (8-ounce) can tomato
   sauce
1½ cups (30 ml) beef stock
2 tablespoons (30 ml) chilli powder
1 tablespoon (15 ml) ground cumin
½ teaspoon ground allspice
340 g (12 ounces) cavatappi
   (corkscrew) pasta

- Sauté beef, onion and garlic in large frypan over medium-high heat for 5 minutes.

- Drain fat and stir in tomatoes, green chilli, beans, tomato sauce, stock, chilli powder, cumin, allspice and a little salt and pepper. Bring mixture to a boil, reduce heat and simmer, for 20 to 25 minutes.

- Cook pasta in saucepan according to package directions, drain and place in 6 soup bowls. Top with beef-tomato mixture and serve immediately. Serves 6.

Cheesy Beefy Gnocchi

455 g (1 pound) lean minced beef
280 g (10 ounces) processed
   cheese spread
1 28-g (10-ounce) can condensed
   tomato soup
2 cups (210 g) gnocchi pasta

- Cook beef in frypan until brown and drain.

- Add soup, cheese spread, 2 cups (500 ml) water and pasta. Bring mixture to a boil.

- Cover and cook over medium heat for 10 to 12 minutes or until pasta is done and stir often. Serves 6.

Chilli with Spaghetti

455 g (1 pound) lean minced beef
2 400-g (14-ounce) cans stewed
   tomatoes
1 425-g (15-ounce) can kidney
   beans, drained
1 230-g (8-ounce) can tomato
   sauce
2 tablespoons (30 ml) chilli powder
2 teaspoons ground cumin
2 teaspoons paprika
230 g (8 ounces) spaghetti pasta,
   cooked, drained
½–1 cup (60–115 g) shredded cheese

- Cook and stir minced beef in large sprayed saucepan or soup pot over medium-high heat until crumbly and brown. Stir in tomatoes, beans, tomato sauce, chilli powder, cumin and a little salt; bring to a boil.

- Reduce heat, cover and simmer for about 15 minutes, stirring occasionally.

- Place cooked pasta in serving bowl and spoon beef-bean mixture over top. Garnish with cheese. Serves 8.

Chilli-Pasta Bowl

340 g (12 ounces) genelli (twisted)
    pasta
1 onion, chopped
1 red capsicum deseeded, chopped
1 tablespoon (15 ml) olive oil
455 g (1 pound) lean minced beef
2 tablespoons (30 ml) chilli powder
1 teaspoon (5 ml) cocoa
1 teaspoon (5 ml) ground cumin
1 teaspoon paprika
1 425-g (15-ounce) can stewed
    tomatoes
1 425-g (15-ounce) can kidney
    beans, rinsed, drained
1 cup (115 g) shredded cheese

- Cook pasta in saucepan according to package directions (drain later). Cook onion and capsicum in oil in frypan over medium-high heat for about 10 minutes or until light brown. Transfer onion mixture to small bowl.

- In same frypan, cook minced beef over medium-high heat until brown and crumbly; discard any fat. Stir in chilli powder, cocoa, cumin and ½ teaspoon salt; cook for 2 minutes.

- Return onion mixture to frypan and stir in tomatoes, paprika, beans and 1 cup (250 ml) water; bring to a boil. Reduce heat to medium, cook for 6 minutes and break up tomatoes with side of spoon.

- Drain pasta and return to saucepan. Add chilli mixture to pasta in saucepan and stir until they blend well. Transfer to serving bowl and sprinkle cheese over top of dish. Serves 6.

Classic Beefy Pasta

680 g (1½ pounds) lean minced beef
2 280-g (10-ounce) cans tomatoes
2 teaspoons minced garlic
230 g (8 ounces) fettuccini (medium egg noodles) pasta
85 g (3 ounces) cream cheese
230 g (8 ounces) sour cream
230 g (8 ounces) shredded cheddar cheese

- Preheat oven to 175° C (350° F).

- Brown beef in frypan. Drain and stir in tomatoes, garlic and a little salt and pepper. Bring to a boil, reduce heat and simmer for 25 minutes.

- While beef mixture cooks, place pasta in large saucepan and cook according to package directions. Drain, stir in cream cheese and stir until cream cheese melts. Fold in sour cream and stir in beef mixture.

- Spoon into sprayed 23 x 33-cm (9 x 13-inch) baking dish. Cover and bake for 30 minutes. Remove from oven, sprinkle cheese over top and return to oven for 5 minutes. Serves 8.

The popular Bolognese sauce originated in Bologna and is made with meat.

Company Beef and Pasta

910 g (2 pounds) lean, minced beef
2 onions, chopped
1 green capsicum, chopped
¾ teaspoon garlic powder
1 400-g (14-ounce) jar spaghetti
    sauce
1 425-g (15-ounce) can Italian
    stewed tomatoes
1 115-g (4-ounce) can sliced
    mushrooms, drained
230 g (8 ounces) rotini
    (short spirals) pasta
750 ml (1½ pints) sour cream
230 g (8 ounces) sliced provolone
    cheese
230 g (8 ounces) shredded
    mozzarella cheese

- Preheat oven to 160° C (325° F).

- Brown and cook beef in deep frypan or soup pot and stir often to break up pieces. Drain off excess fat.

- Add onions, capsicum, garlic powder, spaghetti sauce, stewed tomatoes and mushrooms and mix well. Simmer for 20 minutes.

- Cook pasta in saucepan according to package directions and drain. Pour half of the pasta into sprayed deep 25 x 38-cm (10 x 15-inch) baking dish.

- Cover with half meat-tomato mixture and half sour cream. Top with slices of provolone cheese. Repeat process once more ending with mozzarella cheese.

- Cover and bake for 35 minutes.

- Uncover and continue baking for additional 10 to 15 minutes or until mozzarella cheese melts. Serves 8 to 10.

Delicious Stuffed Shells

24 lumache (large shells) pasta
455 g (1 pound) lean minced beef
1 740-g (26-ounce) can spaghetti sauce
230 g (8 ounces) cream cheese with chives, softened
2 teaspoons dried parsley
230 g (8 ounces) shredded mozzarella cheese
1 cup (100 g) grated parmesan cheese
1 egg, beaten

- Preheat oven to 175° C (350° F).

- Cook pasta in saucepan according to package directions, drain and place on a large sheet of baking paper.

- Cook minced beef in frypan over medium-high heat for about 7 or 8 minutes, stir until crumbly and brown and drain thoroughly. Let cool for about 5 minutes.

- Combine spaghetti sauce and ¼ cup (60 ml) water in large bowl and pour 1 cup (250 ml) in 23 x 33-cm (9 x 13-inch) baking pan.

- In separate bowl, combine cream cheese, parsley, 1½ cups (170 g) mozzarella, ½ cup (50 g) parmesan cheese, egg and cooked beef; mix well.

- Carefully place heaped tablespoonfuls of mixture into each shell and arrange stuffed shells over sauce in baking pan. Pour remaining sauce over top covering shells completely. Cover with foil and bake for 40 minutes.

- Uncover and sprinkle with remaining mozzarella and parmesan cheeses and cook for additional 10 minutes. Serves 8.

Dinner with the Italian Touch

Baked Italian dishes are famous for their rich, flavourful sauces. This recipe is creamy, cheesy and delicious.

910 g (2 pounds) lean minced
    beef
1 onion, chopped
1 red capsicum, chopped
2 teaspoons minced garlic
1 740-g (26-ounce) jar chunky
    spaghetti sauce
2 230-g (8-ounce) jars sliced
    mushrooms, drained
1 teaspoon oregano
2 teaspoons Italian seasoning
340 g (12 ounces) fettuccini
    (medium egg noodles) pasta
425 g (15 ounces) ricotta cheese
500 ml (1 pint) sour cream
145 g (5 ounces) grated parmesan
    cheese
455 g (16 ounces) shredded
    mozzarella cheese

- Preheat oven to 160° C (325° F).

- Brown beef, onion, capsicum and garlic in very large frypan; drain well. Add spaghetti sauce, mushrooms, oregano, Italian seasoning and dash of salt and pepper. Heat to a boil, reduce heat and simmer about 15 minutes.

- Cook pasta in saucepan according to package directions and drain.

- Combine ricotta cheese, sour cream, parmesan cheese and half mozzarella cheese in large bowl.

- Layer half pasta, half beef mixture and half cheese mixture in sprayed 25 x 38-cm (10 x 15-inch) baking dish. Repeat layers.

- Cover and bake for 40 minutes. Remove covering and sprinkle with remaining mozzarella cheese. Bake for additional 5 to 10 minutes. Serves 20.

Family OK Casserole

680 g (1½ pounds) lean minced beef
2 425-g (15-ounce) cans stewed
**   tomatoes**
2 green chillies, chopped
340 g (12 ounces) tagliatelle
**   (thin egg noodles) pasta**
230 g (8 ounces) cream cheese,
**   softened**
230 g (8 ounces) light
**   sour cream**
455 g (16 ounces) shredded
**   mozzarella cheese, divided**

- Preheat oven to 175° C (350° F).

- Brown beef in large saucepan on medium heat and drain fat. Add stewed tomatoes and green chillies; reduce heat and simmer 20 minutes.

- Cook pasta in saucepan according to package directions and drain. Beat cream cheese in bowl until smooth, add sour cream and mix until they blend well.

- Spread half pasta into sprayed 23 x 33-cm (9 x 13-inch) baking pan. Cover with half cream cheese mixture and half mozzarella cheese. Spread all meat-tomato mixture over cheese.

- Layer remaining pasta, cream cheese mixture and cheese. Cover and bake for 35 minutes. Let stand for 10 minutes before serving. Serves 12.

Fettuccini Italian

*Adding broccoli to this classic
Italian recipe dresses it up
and adds wonderful flavour.*

170 g (6 ounces) fettuccini (medium
    egg noodles) pasta
230 g (½ pound) lean minced beef
1 teaspoon minced garlic
1 onion, minced
1 230-g (8-ounce) can tomato
    sauce
1 425-g (15-ounce) can Italian
    stewed tomatoes, with liquid
1 teaspoon Italian seasoning
2 eggs
2 tablespoons (30 g) butter
230 g (8 ounces) shredded
    mozzarella cheese
1 cup (230 g) cottage cheese
1 cup (225 g) chopped fresh
    broccoli, stemmed
1 145-g (5-ounce) package grated
    parmesan cheese

- Preheat oven to 175° C (350° F).

- Cook pasta in saucepan according
  to package directions, drain and set
  aside.

- Brown beef in large frypan and stir
  to crumble. Add garlic and onion,
  stir to mix and reduce heat. Cook
  for 5 minutes.

- Add tomato sauce, stewed
  tomatoes with liquid and Italian
  seasoning. Stir and bring to boil.
  Reduce heat, cover and simmer
  for 10 to 12 minutes, stirring
  occasionally.

- Beat 1 egg and melted butter in
  mixing bowl. Stir in pasta and
  mozzarella cheese.

- Spoon mixture into deep 25-cm
  (10-inch) dish and press down on
  bottom and sides to pack fettuccini
  mixture.

- In separate bowl, mix remaining
  egg and cottage cheese. Pour over
  pasta in dish and smooth over
  surface. Sprinkle with broccoli.

- Spoon beef mixture evenly over
  top. Sprinkle parmesan evenly over
  top and remove any cheese from
  edges of the dish.

- Bake for 30 minutes or until
  thoroughly hot. Let stand for
  10 minutes to set before cutting.
  Serves 6 to 8.

Garden Spaghetti

340 g (12 ounces) spaghetti pasta
1 tablespoon (15 ml) olive oil
455 g (1 pound) lean minced beef
3 small zucchini, cubed
1 onion, chopped
1 green capsicum, seeded,
    chopped
280 g (10 ounces) frozen
    sliced carrots, thawed
1 teaspoon minced garlic
1 740-g (26-ounce) can chunky
    garden pasta sauce
½ cup (50 g) grated parmesan
    cheese

- Cook pasta in saucepan according to package directions; drain, cover and keep warm.

- Heat oil in large frypan, cook beef for about 5 minutes and stir well to crumble. Stir in zucchini, onion, capsicum, carrots, garlic and a little salt and pepper. Stir occasionally and cook for 10 minutes or until vegetables are tender but crisp.

- Stir in pasta sauce, bring to a boil; reduce heat, simmer for about 8 minutes and stir often. Place warm pasta on serving platter, spoon vegetable-beef sauce over top and sprinkle with parmesan cheese. Serves 8 to 10.

Semolina is the name of the flour most often used in the manufacture of pasta. It is a 'hard' wheat flour made from durum wheat. However, there are also pastas made of spelt, corn or rice, very convenient for those who are gluten intolerant or allergic.

Glorified Spaghetti

230 g (8 ounces) vermicelli
(thin spaghetti) pasta,
broken in half
2 tablespoons (30 ml) olive oil
1 teaspoon minced garlic
2 sticks celery, chopped
680 g (1½ pounds) lean minced
beef
1 teaspoon sugar
2 225-g (8-ounce) cans
tomato sauce
1 170-g (6-ounce) can
tomato paste
230 g (8 ounces) sour cream
85 g (3 ounces) cream cheese,
softened
1 bunch spring onions,
chopped
½ cup (50 g) grated parmesan
cheese

- Preheat oven to 175° C (350° F).

- Cook pasta in saucepan according to package directions; drain and set aside.

- Place oil in large frypan over medium heat and cook garlic, celery, beef, sugar and a little salt and pepper. Cook and stir until beef is no longer pink; drain fat. Add tomato sauce, tomato paste and ¼ cup (60 ml) water and simmer for 15 minutes.

- Beat sour cream and cream cheese in bowl until smooth and stir in spring onions. Spread about ½ cup (125 ml) meat sauce into sprayed 3-L (3-quart) baking dish.

- Layer half pasta, half sour cream mixture and half meat mixture. Repeat layers, cover and bake for 40 minutes.

- Sprinkle parmesan cheese over top of casserole and serve hot. Serves 8.

Hearty Tortellini Bake

2 255-g (9-ounce) refrigerated
   cheese tortellini pasta
455 g (1 pound) lean minced beef
1 small onion, chopped
2 teaspoons minced garlic
1 teaspoon dried oregano
1 740-g (26-ounce) can chunky
   spaghetti sauce with herbs
3 small zucchini, cut in thick slices
½ cup (50 g) grated parmesan
   cheese

- Cook pasta in saucepan according to package directions and drain.

- Cook beef, onion and garlic in large frypan on medium-high heat. Add oregano, spaghetti sauce and zucchini slices and bring to a boil. Reduce heat to medium-low and cook for about 15 minutes, stirring occasionally.

- Transfer half of the pasta into sprayed 23 x 33-cm (9 x 13-inch) baking dish and top with half sauce and half cheese. Repeat layers. Serves 3 to 4.

Cooked pasta does not freeze well, but baked casseroles which include pasta can be frozen.

Impressive Baked Ziti

455 g (16 ounces) ziti (thin tubes)
   pasta
1 tablespoon (15 ml) olive oil
1 large onion, chopped
1 red capsicum, seeded, chopped
455 g (1 pound) lean minced beef
1 tablespoon (15 ml) minced garlic
1 740-g (26-ounce) jar pasta sauce
230 g (8 ounces) shredded
   mozzarella cheese,
425 g (15 ounces) ricotta
280 g (10 ounces) frozen spinach,
   thawed, well drained*

- Preheat oven to 190° C (375° F).

- Cook pasta in saucepan according to package directions; drain and keep warm.

- Place oil, onion, capsicum, beef and garlic in soup pot over medium heat. Cook for 10 to 15 minutes, stirring often or until there is no trace of pink in beef.

- Add pasta sauce and heat 5 minutes. Stir pasta into beef-onion mixture and toss to coat. Add half mozzarella cheese, ricotta and spinach and toss again.

- Spread mixture into sprayed 23 x 33-cm (9 x 13-inch) baking dish, cover and bake for 15 minutes. Uncover and sprinkle remaining mozzarella cheese over top and return to oven for 5 minutes. Serves 10 to 12.

TIP: Squeeze spinach between paper towels to completely remove excess moisture.

Italian Dinner

Baked Italian dishes are famous for their rich, flavourful sauces. This recipe tastes wonderful on the first night and is even better the next day served as leftovers.

910 g (2 pounds) lean minced beef
1 onion, chopped
1 red capsicum, seeded, chopped
2 sticks celery, chopped
2 garlic cloves, finely minced
1 910-g (32-ounce) jar
    spaghetti sauce
3 170-g (6-ounce) jars sliced
    mushrooms, drained
½ teaspoon oregano
1 teaspoon Italian seasoning
230 g (8 ounces) fettuccini (medium
    egg noodles) pasta
230 g (8 ounces) cream cheese,
    softened
500-ml (1-pint) carton sour cream
1 cup (100 g) grated parmesan
    cheese
455 g (16 ounces) shredded
    mozzarella cheese

- Preheat oven to 160° C (325° F).

- Brown beef, onion, capsicum, celery and garlic in very large frypan and drain well.

- Add spaghetti sauce, mushrooms, oregano, Italian seasoning and dash of salt and pepper. Heat to boiling, turn heat down and simmer for about 15 minutes.

- Cook pasta in saucepan according to package directions and drain.

- Beat cream cheese in bowl until creamy and add sour cream and cheeses.

- Layer half pasta, half beef mixture and half cheeses in sprayed deep 25 x 38-cm (10 x 15-inch) baking dish. Repeat layers.

- Cover and bake for 30 minutes. Remove covering and bake for additional 10 to 15 minutes. Serves 10 to 12.

Italian Manicotti

455 g (1 pound) lean minced beef
2 teaspoons minced garlic
2 onions, chopped
1 795-g (28-ounce) can diced
  tomatoes with juice
230 g (8 ounces) fresh mushrooms,
  sliced
1 teaspoon fennel seeds
2 teaspoons basil
1 teaspoon Italian seasoning
2 280-g (10-ounce) frozen
  spinach, thawed
½ cup (50 g) grated parmesan
  cheese, divided
455 g (16 ounces) cottage cheese
¼ teaspoon ground nutmeg
14 manicotti (large tubes)
  pasta, cooked al dente

- Preheat oven to 160° C (325° F).

- Brown minced beef in large frypan, add garlic and onion and reduce heat to low. Simmer for 10 minutes and drain.

- Add tomatoes with juice, mushrooms, fennel seeds, basil, Italian seasoning, ½ teaspoon each of salt and pepper and stir to mix well. Bring to a boil, reduce heat and simmer for 10 minutes, stir occasionally.

- Squeeze spinach between paper towels to completely remove excess moisture.

- Combine spinach, half parmesan, cottage cheese, nutmeg and ½ teaspoon pepper in bowl.

- Spoon about one-third of beef sauce evenly in sprayed 23 x 33-cm (9 x 13-inch) baking dish.

- Fill cooked pasta shells with spinach mixture and place on beef layer in baking dish. Repeat until all spinach mixture is in manicotti shells.

- Pour remaining beef sauce evenly over pasta shells to cover. Sprinkle remaining parmesan cheese over top.

- Cover and bake for 1 hour 30 minutes or until shells are tender. Serves 8 to 12.

Lasagna Roll Ups

12 lasagna sheets
455 g (1 pound) lean minced beef
1 onion, finely chopped
1 400-g (14-ounce) jar spaghetti
    sauce
425 g (15 ounces) ricotta cheese
280 g (10 ounces) frozen, chopped
    spinach, thawed, drained
1½ cups (175 g) shredded
    mozzarella cheese

- Preheat oven to 175° C (350° F).

- Cook lasagna sheets according to package directions and drain.

- Cook beef and onion in frypan on high for about 3 minutes, stirring constantly, drain.

- Stir in spaghetti sauce and heat to boiling, stirring constantly. Pour into 18 x 28-cm (7 x 11-inch) baking pan.

- Mix ricotta cheese, spinach, 1 cup (115 g) mozzarella cheese and a little salt and pepper. Spread 3 tablespoons (20 g) cheese-spinach mixture over each lasagna sheet. Roll each lasagna sheet; cut roll crosswise in half.

- Place rolls, cut-side down in beef mixture. Cover and bake for about 30 minutes. To serve, sprinkle with remaining cheese. Serves 6 to 8.

The word 'lasagna' *(or* lasagne*) actually means 'cooking pot' in Italian.*

Mac Cheese Dinner

680 g (1½ pounds) lean minced
  beef
2 200-g (7-ounce) macaroni and
  cheese dinners
1 425-g (15-ounce) can corn kernels,
  drained
1½ cups (175 g) shredded Colby
  cheese

- Sprinkle minced beef with
  1 teaspoon salt in large frypan,
  brown until no longer
  pink and drain.

- Prepare pasta and cheese
  in saucepan according to
  package directions.

- Spoon in beef, pasta and corn in
  sprayed 5-L (5-quart) slow cooker
  and mix well.

- Cover and cook on low for
  4 to 5 hours.

- When ready to serve, sprinkle
  cheese over top and leave in cooker
  until cheese melts. Serves 4 to 6.

Quick Skillet Dinner

680 g (1½ pounds) lean minced
  beef
⅔ cup (150 ml) stir-fry sauce
455 g (16 ounces) frozen stir-fry
  vegetables
170 g (6 ounces) Oriental-flavoured
  ramen noodles

- Brown and crumble minced beef in
  large frypan. Add 2⅓ cups (575 ml)
  water, stir-fry sauce, vegetables and
  both seasoning packets contained in
  noodle package.

- Cook and stir on medium heat for
  about 5 minutes.

- Break up noodles, add to beef-
  vegetable mixture and cook for
  about 6 minutes. Stir to separate
  noodles as they soften. Serve hot.
  Serves 4 to 6.

Make-Believe Lasagna

455 g (1 pound) lean minced beef
1 onion, chopped
½ teaspoon garlic powder
1 510-g (18-ounce) can
    spaghetti sauce
½ teaspoon (2 ml) oregano
6–8 lasagna sheets
340 g (12 ounces) cottage cheese
½ cup (50 g) grated parmesan
    cheese
340 g (12 ounces) shredded
    mozzarella cheese

- Brown minced beef and onion in large frypan. Add garlic powder, spaghetti sauce and oregano. Cook just until thoroughly warm.

- Spoon layer of meat sauce in sprayed, oval slow cooker. Add layer of lasagna sheets (break to fit slow cooker).

- Top with layer of half remaining meat sauce, half cottage cheese, half parmesan cheese and half mozzarella cheese. Repeat layers and start with more lasagna sheets.

- Cover and cook on low for 6 to 8 hours. Serves 4 to 6.

The ancient Romans made a kind of lasagna called lagane. This was baked, rather than boiled.

Mexican Beef and Pasta

This is ideal to make ahead of time for a quick and easy supper and it will serve about 14 people. These blended flavours create a delicious dish that people always remember.

680–910 g (1½–2 pounds) lean minced beef
1 onion, chopped
1 green capsicum, chopped
455 g (16 ounces) cubed processed cheese
280 g (10 ounces) can cream of celery soup
2 425-g (15-ounce) cans stewed tomatoes
2 green chillies, chopped
1 230-g (8-ounce) can corn kernels, drained
½ teaspoon chilli powder
¼ teaspoon ground mustard
230 g (8 ounces) fettuccini (medium egg noodles) pasta
¼ cup (60 g) butter, cut into 4–5 slices
1 cup (115 g) shredded cheddar cheese

- Preheat oven to 175° C (350° F).

- Cook minced beef, onion and capsicum in frypan until beef is no longer pink and vegetables are tender. Drain.

- Remove from heat, add processed cheese and stir until cheese melts.

- Combine, stewed tomatoes, green chillies, corn, chilli powder, mustard and 1½ teaspoons salt and ½ teaspoon pepper in large bowl. Add beef mixture and mix well.

- Cook pasta in saucepan according to package directions and drain well.

- While pasta is still very hot, add butter and stir until it melts.

- Stir pasta in with tomato-beef mixture. Transfer to sprayed 25 x 38-cm (10 x 15-inch) baking dish.

- Cover and bake for 45 minutes. Uncover and sprinkle cheese over casserole and return to oven for 4 to 10 minutes. Serves 14.

Oriental Beef and Noodles

455 g (1 pound) lean minced beef
170 g (6 ounces) Oriental ramen
    noodles, crumbled
455 g (16 ounces) frozen stir-fry
    vegetables
280 g (10 ounces) frozen green peas,
    thawed
¼ teaspoon ground ginger
3 fresh spring onions,
    thinly sliced

- Cook beef in large frypan over
  medium heat for 6 minutes or until
  no longer pink. Stir in 1 flavouring
  packet from ramen noodles and mix
  well. Transfer to warm plate.

- In same frypan, combine stir-fry
  vegetables, peas, ginger, noodles,
  2⅔ cups (650 ml) water and
  remaining flavouring packet.
  Bring to boil. Reduce heat,
  cover and simmer 5 minutes,
  stirring occasionally.

- Return beef to frypan and cook
  for additional 3 minutes or until
  thoroughly hot. Just before serving,
  stir in sliced onions. Serves 8.

Pasta-Beef Skillet

455 g (1 pound) lean minced beef
1 small onion, chopped
1 teaspoon minced garlic
1 425-g (15-ounce) can Italian
    stewed tomatoes
340 g (12 ounces) penne (tube) pasta
230 g (8 ounces) shredded cheddar
    cheese
1 cup (55 g) crushed corn chips

- Cook beef, onion and garlic in
  large sprayed frypan over medium-
  high heat, stirring often, until
  beef is crumbly and brown. Stir in
  tomatoes, 1 cup (250 ml) water and
  pasta. Cover and cook for about
  15 minutes or until pasta is tender.

- Sprinkle cheese over top, cover
  and cook over medium-low heat
  just until cheese melts. Sprinkle
  with chips and serve immediately.
  Serves 8.

Peanuts, Beef and Snowpeas

230 g (8 ounces) capelli d'angelo
   (angel hair) pasta
455 g (1 pound) lean minced beef
1 small onion, finely chopped
2 sticks celery, cut in 2.5-cm
   (1-inch) pieces
1 red capsicum, seeded, julienned
230 g (8 ounces) frozen snowpeas,
   thawed
½ litre (14 ounces) chicken stock
¼ teaspoon cayenne pepper
1 tablespoon (15 ml) cornflour
½ cup (145 g) peanut butter
⅓ cup (55 g) chopped, salted
   peanuts

- Cook pasta in saucepan according to package directions, drain and keep warm.

- Cook beef over medium-high heat for 7 minutes, stir until crumbly and drain. Add onion, celery, capsicum and snowpeas. Cook and stir for 4 minutes or until vegetables are tender but crisp.

- Combine stock, cayenne pepper and cornflour in saucepan. Cook and stir on medium heat until slightly thick. Stir in cooked beef, vegetables and peanut butter. Cook for 2 minutes, stirring frequently, until thick and bubbly.

- Place pasta in serving plate, spoon beef-vegetable mixture over pasta and sprinkle top with peanuts. Serves 6 to 8.

Ravioli and More

455 g (1 pound) lean minced beef
1 teaspoon (5 ml) garlic powder
1 large onion, chopped
2 zucchini, grated
¼ cup (60 g) butter
1 795-g (28-ounce) jar spaghetti
   sauce
710 g (25 ounces) mushroom-filled
   ravioli, cooked
340 g (12 ounces) shredded
   mozzarella cheese

- Preheat oven to 175° C (350° F).

- Brown minced beef in large frypan until no longer pink and drain. Add garlic powder and ½ teaspoon each of salt and pepper.

- Cook onion and zucchini with butter in saucepan just until tender but crisp and stir in spaghetti sauce.

- Spread ½ cup (125 ml) sauce in sprayed 23 x 33-cm (9 x 13-inch) baking dish. Layer half of pasta, half spaghetti sauce, half beef and half cheese. Repeat layers, but omit remaining cheese. Cover and bake for 35 minutes.

- Uncover and sprinkle remaining cheese. Let stand for 10 minutes before serving. Serves 8.

Historians believe that the Etruscans were making pasta of spelt wheat as early as 400 B.C. The Etruscans lived in central and northern Italy before the founding of Rome.

Seriously Good Stuffed Rigatoni

230 g (8 ounces) rigatoni
   (large tubes) pasta
280 g (10 ounces) cheddar cheese
455 g (1 pound) lean minced beef
1 425-g (15-ounce) jar spaghetti
   sauce
½ cup (60 g) shredded mozzarella
   cheese
½ cup (60 g) seasoned
   breadcrumbs

- Preheat oven to 175° C (350° F).

- Cook pasta in saucepan according to package directions. Drain, rinse thoroughly and place on baking tray covered with baking paper. Cut cheese into strips about 3 x 0.6 cm (1¼ x ¼ inch). Insert strip of cheese in each cooked pasta tube and place in sprayed 2-L (2-quart) baking dish.

- Brown beef in non-stick frypan, stirring often, for about 10 minutes. Stir in spaghetti sauce and heat on medium-high until thoroughly hot. Pour over stuffed pasta and sprinkle mozzarella cheese over top.

- Cover and bake for 20 minutes. Uncover and sprinkle breadcrumbs over top and return to oven for 10 minutes. Serves 8.

Simple Spaghetti Bake

230 g (8 ounces) spaghetti pasta
455 g (1 pound) lean minced beef
1 green capsicum, finely chopped
1 onion, chopped
1 280-g (10-ounce) can condensed
  tomato soup
1 425-g (15-ounce) can tomato
  sauce
2 teaspoons Italian seasoning
1 230-g (8-ounce) can corn kernels,
  drained
1 115-g (4-ounce) can black
  sliced olives, drained
340 g (12 ounces) shredded
  cheddar cheese

- Cook pasta in saucepan according to package directions, drain and set aside.

- Cook beef, capsicum and onion in frypan and drain.

- Add remaining ingredients, ⅓ cup (75 ml) water and ½ teaspoon salt and pasta to beef mixture and stir well. Pour into sprayed 23 x 33-cm (9 x 13-inch) baking dish and cover.

- Refrigerate for 2 to 3 hours.

- When ready to bake, preheat oven to 175° C (350° F).

- Cover and bake for 45 minutes. Serves 8 to 10.

Skillet Beef and Pasta

230 g (8 ounces) rotini (spiral) pasta
½ litre (14 ounces) beef stock
455 g (1 pound) lean minced beef
2 310-g (11-ounce) cans
    corn kernels, drained
½ red capsicum, seeded, finely
    chopped
½ green capsicum, seeded, finely
    chopped
455 g (16 ounces) cubed processed
    cheese
1 teaspoon paprika

- Cook pasta in saucepan according to package directions and substitute beef stock for 1¾ cups (425 ml) water.

- While pasta cooks, brown beef in large frypan and drain.

- Stir in corn, capsicum, paprika and cheese and cook on low heat until cheese melts. Gently stir cooked pasta into beef mixture until pasta coats well. Spoon mixture into serving bowl and garnish with sprigs of parsley, if desired. Serves 8.

Spicy Spaghetti

680 g (1½ pounds) lean minced beef
2½ teaspoons chilli powder
1 425-g (15-ounce) can tomato
    sauce
200 g (7 ounces) spaghetti pasta
1 heaped tablespoon (15 ml) beef
    seasoning
Shredded cheddar cheese

- Brown beef in frypan until no longer pink. Place in 4 to 5-L (4 to 5-quart) slow cooker.

- Add chilli powder, tomato sauce, pasta, 2⅓ cups (575 ml) water and beef seasoning and mix well.

- Cover and cook on low for 6 to 7 hours.

- When ready to serve, cover with lots of shredded cheddar cheese. Serves 4 to 6.

Skillet Lasagna

680 g (1½ pounds) lean minced
    beef
1 onion, finely chopped
2 teaspoons minced garlic
1 740-g (26-ounce) jar spaghetti
    sauce
5 lasagna sheets, broken
    into 5-cm (2-inch) pieces
425 g (15 ounces) ricotta cheese
2 eggs, beaten
½ cup (50 g) grated parmesan
    cheese
2 teaspoons dried parsley
230 g (8 ounces) shredded
    mozzarella cheese

- Cook beef, onion and garlic in large nonstick frypan over medium-high heat for about 8 minutes, stirring occasionally, until beef is thoroughly cooked; drain.

- Stir in spaghetti sauce, 1 cup (250 ml) water and lasagna sheets. Reduce heat to medium-low. Cover and cook for about 20 minutes, stirring often, until lasagna sheets are almost tender.

- Combine ricotta cheese, 2 tablespoons (30 ml) water, eggs, parmesan cheese and parsley in bowl. Spread over partially cooked pasta mixture.

- Sprinkle with half mozzarella cheese, cover and cook for additional 10 to 15 minutes or until cottage cheese mixture sets and pasta is tender.

- Sprinkle with remaining cheese and serve right from the frypan. Serves 8.

Spaghetti Pizza Special

170 g (6 ounces) spaghetti pasta,
  cooked, drained
⅓ cup (25 g) grated parmesan
  cheese
1 egg, beaten
1 cup (225 g) cottage cheese,
455 g (1 pound) lean minced beef
½ cup (80 g) chopped onion
1 425-g (15-ounce) can tomato
  sauce
1 teaspoon minced garlic
1 teaspoon dried oregano
1 tablespoon (15 ml) sugar
½ cup (60 g) mozzarella cheese

- Preheat oven to 175° C (350° F).

- Mix pasta while still warm with parmesan and egg in large bowl.

- Spoon into sprayed 25-cm (10-inch) round pan (or pizza pan) and pat mixture up and around sides with spoon to form crust. Spoon cottage cheese over pasta layer.

- Brown meat and onion in frypan. Drain and add tomato sauce, garlic, oregano, sugar and a little salt and pepper. Simmer for 15 minutes.

- Spoon meat mixture over cottage cheese and bake for 30 minutes. Sprinkle mozzarella on top and return to oven for 5 minutes or just until cheese melts. To serve, cut into wedges. Serves 8.

If the water is not at a full rolling boil when the pasta is added, the outside of the pasta will not 'set' and the pasta will be mushy.

Spicy Beef and Pasta

This is an ideal casserole to make ahead of time for a quick-and-easy dinner. The flavours blend to create a delicious dish that people will always remember.

910 g (2 pounds) lean minced beef
1 large onion, chopped
1 green capsicum, seeded, chopped
455 g (16 ounces) shredded processed cheese
1 280-g (10-ounce) can cream of celery soup
1 425-g (15-ounce) can stewed tomatoes
1 425-g (15-ounce) can corn kernels, drained
1 teaspoon chilli powder
340 g (12 ounces) fettuccini (medium egg noodles) pasta
230 g (8 ounces) shredded cheddar cheese

- Preheat oven to 175° C (350° F).

- Cook beef, onion and capsicum in frypan until beef is no longer pink and vegetables are tender. Drain. Remove from heat, add processed cheese and stir until cheese melts.

- Combine soup, stewed tomatoes, corn, chilli powder and a little salt in large mixing bowl. Add beef mixture and mix well.

- Cook pasta in saucepan according to package directions and drain well. Stir pasta into tomato-beef mixture. Transfer to sprayed 25 x 30-cm (10 x 15-inch) baking dish.

- Cover and bake for 50 to 55 minutes.

- Uncover and sprinkle cheddar cheese over casserole and return to oven for 5 minutes. Serves 20.

Spicy Beef Fettuccini

455 g (1 pound) lean minced beef
30 g (1 ounce) taco seasoning mix
1 425-g (15-ounce) can stewed
**   tomatoes**
1 teaspoon paprika
1 425-g (15-ounce) can borlotti
**   beans with liquid**
455 g (16 ounces) fettuccini
**   (medium egg noodles) pasta**
1 bunch fresh spring onions,
**   sliced**

- Cook beef in large frypan and drain. Add taco seasoning with ½ cup (125 ml) water and simmer for 15 minutes.

- Stir in stewed tomatoes, beans and a little salt and pepper.

- Cook pasta in saucepan according to package directions and place on serving platter. Spoon spicy beef over pasta and sprinkle with sliced spring onions. Serves 8.

Yummy Creamy Pasta

570 g (1¼ pounds) lean minced beef
1 onion, chopped
Garlic salt
1 280-g (10-ounce) can cream of
**   celery soup**
340 g (12 ounces) macaroni and
**   cheese sauce**

- Brown beef and onion in frypan and stir until beef crumbles.

- Add a little pepper and garlic salt, if desired. Add soup and mix.

- Prepare pasta and cheese in saucepan according to package directions. Stir into beef mixture.

- Simmer for 20 minutes. Serve hot. Serves 8.

Spinach Manicotti

230 g (8 ounces) manicotti (large tubes) pasta

280 g (10 ounces) frozen chopped spinach, thawed, drained

455 g (1 pound) lean minced beef

1 teaspoon (5 ml) dried onion flakes

1 cup (115 g) shredded mozzarella cheese

½ cup (250 g) pesto

1 egg

1 740-g (26-ounce) jar tomato pasta sauce

- Preheat oven to 190° C (375° F).

- Cook pasta according to package directions; drain and rinse with cold water. Place pasta on large piece of baking paper to cool.

- Combine spinach, beef, onion flakes, cheese, pesto, egg and a little salt and pepper in bowl.

- Fill each pasta tube by carefully stuffing beef-spinach mixture into each tube. Place pasta on sprayed 23 x 33-cm (9 x 13-inch) glass baking dish. Pour pasta sauce over pasta.

- Cover and bake for 35 to 40 minutes or until filling is no longer pink in centre. Serves 8.

Asian Beef and Noodles

680 g (1½ pounds) lean minced beef
170 g (6 ounces) Oriental-flavoured ramen noodles
455 g (16 ounces) frozen Oriental stir-fry vegetables, thawed
½ teaspoon ground ginger
1 bunch fresh spring onions, sliced

- Cook beef in large frypan and drain. Add ½ cup (125 ml) water and simmer 10 minutes. Transfer to separate bowl.

- In same frypan, combine 2 cups (500 ml) water, broken up noodles, vegetables, ginger and both seasoning packets from ramen noodles. Bring to a boil, reduce heat, cover and simmer for 3 minutes, stirring occasionally.

- Return beef to frypan and stir in spring onions. Serve right from frypan. Serves 8.

Beef and Macaroni Dinner

280 g (10 ounces) tube pasta, cooked, drained
3 tablespoons (45 ml) olive oil
680 g (1½ pounds) lean minced beef, browned, drained
1 onion, chopped
3 sticks celery, chopped
2 280-g (10-ounce) cans tomato soup
1 170-g (6-ounce) can tomato paste
1 beef stock cube
230 g (8 ounces) cubed cheddar cheese

- Toss cooked pasta with oil to make sure it does not stick.

- Place in sprayed slow cooker.

- Add beef, onion, celery, tomato soup, tomato paste, beef stock cube and ⅔ cup (150 ml) water and stir to mix well.

- Cover and cook on low for 4 to 6 hours. Before last hour of cooking time, stir in cubed cheese. Serves 4 to 6.

Beef and Mushrooms over Spaghetti

455 g (1 pound) lean minced beef
3 tablespoons (45 ml) olive oil
1 onion, chopped
1 cup (150 g) chopped green capsicum
230 g (8 ounces) mushrooms, sliced
2 teaspoons (10 ml) minced garlic
1 425-g (15-ounce) can stewed tomatoes
1 230-g (8-ounce) can tomato paste
340 g (12 ounces) vermicelli (thin spaghetti) pasta
⅓ cup (35 g) grated parmesan cheese

- Cook beef in large frypan over medium-high heat for 4 to 5 minutes; break up lumps with fork. Remove beef from frypan with slotted spoon and set aside. Discard pan drippings.

- Heat oil on medium-high heat and cook onion, capsicum, mushrooms and garlic for about 5 minutes; stir often.

- Return beef to frypan and stir in stewed tomatoes, tomato paste, ¼ cup (60 ml) water and a little salt and pepper. Bring to a boil, reduce heat to low and simmer sauce for 30 minutes, stirring occasionally.

- While sauce simmers, cook pasta in saucepan according to package directions; drain and place in serving dish. Spoon beef sauce over pasta and top with grated parmesan cheese. Serves 6 to 8.

Strand pastas like spaghetti and stickbon pastas like linguine are great with sauces.

Beef and Fettuccini

1.4 kg (3 pounds) lean beef, cubed
2 280-g (10-ounce) cans mushroom
  soup
½ cup (125 ml) cooking sherry
30 g (1 ounce) onion soup
   mix
Fettuccini (medium egg
   noodles) pasta, cooked

- Preheat oven to 160° C (325° F).

- Mix all ingredients and add ¾ cup (175 ml) water.

- Pour into 3-L (3-quart) baking dish.

- Bake for about 2 hours. Serve over pasta. Serves 8.

Spiced Beef

455 g (1 pound) lean minced beef
30 g (1 ounce) taco seasoning mix
1 455-g (16-ounce) can stewed
   tomatoes with liquid
1 teaspoon paprika
1 455-g (16-ounce) can kidney
   beans with liquid
455 g (1 pound) linguine (thin egg
   noodles) pasta

- Cook beef in frypan and drain. Add taco seasoning and ½ cup (125 ml) water and simmer for 15 minutes.

- Add stewed tomatoes, paprika and kidney beans. (You may need to add ¼ teaspoon/1 ml salt.)

- Cook pasta in saucepan according to package directions and serve beef over the pasta. Serves 6.

Beef and Pasta al Grande

680 g (1½ pounds) lean minced
 beef
1 onion, chopped
1 red capsicum, chopped
2 425-g (15-ounce) cans stewed
 tomatoes with liquid
1 teaspoon paprika
2 425-g (15-ounce) cans corn
 kernels, drained
230 g (8 ounces) fettuccini (medium
 egg noodles) pasta
5 cups (570 g) shredded cheddar
 cheese

- Brown beef in frypan and drain fat.

- Place beef in sprayed 5 to 6-L
 (5 to 6-quart) slow cooker, add
 onions and capsicum, cheese,
 tomatoes, corn and about
 1 teaspoon (5 ml) salt and mix well.

- Cover and cook on low for
 4 to 5 hours.

- Cook pasta in saucepan according
 to package directions, drain and
 fold into beef-tomato mixture.
 Cook for additional 30 minutes to
 heat thoroughly.

- When ready to serve, top with
 cheddar cheese, several sprinkles of
 chopped fresh parsley or chopped
 fresh spring onions. Serves 4 to 6.

*The Chinese were making noodles, one of
the two forms of pasta, by 2000 B.C.*

Spaghetti and Meatballs

510 g (18 ounces) frozen meatballs,
   thawed
1 795-g (28-ounce) jar spaghetti
   sauce
230 g (8 ounces) spaghetti pasta
145 g (5 ounces) fresh shredded
   parmesan cheese

- Heat meatballs and pasta sauce on high in large microwave-safe dish for 10 to 12 minutes. Stir twice.

- Cook pasta in saucepan according to package directions and drain well. Pour onto serving plate and spoon meatball sauce over pasta. Top with cheese. Serves 4 to 5.

Meatballs and Orzo Casserole

1 onion, chopped
1 red capsicum, chopped
2 sticks celery, sliced
2 tablespoons (30 ml) Italian salad
   dressing
½-litre (14-ounce) carton beef stock
1 cup (105 g) orzo (tiny) pasta
18 cooked, frozen meatballs
2 tomatoes, chopped, drained
1 teaspoon dried parsley
⅓ cup (35 g) grated parmesan
   cheese

- Stir-fry vegetables and dressing in large sprayed frypan over medium-high heat for about 2 minutes.

- Add stock and heat to boiling. Stir in pasta and meatballs and bring to a boil. Cover and cook for 10 minutes, stirring occasionally.

- Stir in tomatoes and parsley; cover and cook for additional 5 minutes or until most of liquid absorbs and pasta is tender. Spoon into serving bowl and top with parmesan cheese. Serves 6.

Beef over Pasta

910 g (2 pounds) lean beef stew
    meat
2 cups (320 g) shallots, peeled
1 green capsicum
1 170-g (6-ounce) jar pitted Greek
    olives or black olives
½ cup (30 g) sun-dried tomatoes
    in oil, drained, chopped
1 795-g (28-ounce) jar tomato pasta
    sauce
230 g (8 ounces) cavatappi
    (corkscrew) pasta

- Place beef and onions in sprayed
  4 or 5-L (4 to 5-quart) slow cooker.

- Cut capsicum in 1-inch (2.5-cm)
  cubes and add to slow cooker.

- Add olives, tomatoes and
  capsicum and pour tomato pasta
  sauce over top.

- Cover and cook on low for
  8 to 10 hours.

- Serve over hot, cooked pasta.
  Serves 4 to 6.

Beef and Gravy

910 g (2 pounds) sirloin steak or
    thick round steak
Olive oil
30 g (1 ounce) onion soup mix
1 280-g (10-ounce) can mushroom
    soup
1 115-g (4-ounce) can sliced
    mushrooms, drained
Fettuccini (medium egg
    noodles) pasta, cooked

- Cut steak in ½-inch (1.2-cm)
  pieces. Brown beef in frypan in a
  little oil and place in 5 to 6-L
  (5 to 6-quart) slow cooker.

- Combine onion soup mix,
  mushroom soup, mushrooms and
  ½ cup (125 ml) water and mix well.
  Spoon over top of beef.

- Cover and cook on low for
  7 to 8 hours. Serve over pasta.
  Serves 4 to 6.

Beef
over Fettuccini

1.4 kg (3 pounds) sirloin beef
½ cup (70 g) plus 3 tablespoons
**   flour**
230 g (8 ounces) fresh mushrooms,
**   sliced**
1 bunch fresh spring onions,
**   chopped**
1 small red capsicum,
**   seeded, chopped**
¼ cup (70 g) tomato sauce
½-litre (14-ounce) carton beef stock
1 tablespoon (15 ml) Worcestershire
**   sauce**
340 g (12 ounces) fettuccini (medium
**   egg noodles) pasta, cooked**

- Coat beef with ½ cup (60 g) flour in bowl and transfer to sprayed slow cooker.

- Add mushrooms, onion, capsicum, tomato sauce, stock, Worcestershire sauce and a little salt and pepper.

- Cover and cook on low for 8 to 9 hours. About 1 hour before serving, turn heat to high.

- Combine remaining flour with ¼ cup (60 ml) water in small bowl, stir into cooker and cook until liquid thickens.

- Serve over hot pasta. Serves 6 to 8.

Pasta lisce *refers to pasta with a smooth finish.*

Beef and Mushrooms Supreme

2 280-g (10-ounce) cans
    mushroom soup
½-litre (14-ounce) carton
    beef stock
2 beef stock cubes
2 115-g (4-ounce) cans sliced
    mushrooms, drained
910 g (2 pounds) round steak
Fettuccini (medium egg
    noodles) pasta, cooked
Butter
230 g (8 ounces) sour cream

- Combine soups, beef stock, beef stock cubes and sliced mushrooms in bowl. Place in slow cooker and stir to blend.

- Add slices of beef and stir well.

- Cover and cook on low for 4 to 5 hours.

- When ready to serve, cook pasta, drain, add salt and a little butter.

- Stir sour cream into sauce in slow cooker. Spoon sauce and beef over pasta. Serves 4 to 6.

Thomas Jefferson introduced pasta to the United States.
He discovered it when visiting Italy while he was serving
as ambassador to France. He purchased a pasta-making machine
and a shipment of macaroni to go to his home in the United States.

Thai Beef, Noodles and Veggies

260 g (8.8 ounces) Thai-flavoured noodles
455 g (1 pound) sirloin steak, cut in strips
Olive oil
455 g (16 ounces) frozen stir-fry vegetables, thawed
½ cup (85 g) chopped peanuts

- Cook noodles in saucepan according to package directions, remove from heat and cover.

- Season sirloin strips with a little salt and pepper.

- Brown half sirloin strips in a little oil in frypan and cook for about 2 minutes. Remove from frypan and drain. Brown remaining sirloin strips in frypan with a little oil and cook for about 2 minutes. Remove from frypan and drain.

- In same frypan, place vegetables and ½ cup (125 ml) water, cover and cook for 5 minutes or until tender but crisp.

- Remove from heat, add steak strips and toss to mix. To serve, sprinkle with chopped peanuts. Serves 6 to 8.

Stroganoff over Spinach Pasta

340 g (12 ounces) spinach
    fettuccini (medium egg
    noodles) pasta
2 tablespoons (30 ml) olive oil
680 g (1½ pounds) sirloin steak,
    sliced in thin strips
230 g (8 ounces) mushrooms
1 small onion, finely chopped
28 g (1 ounce) brown gravy mix
¼ cup (60 ml) white wine
230 g (8 ounces) sour cream
1 teaspoon dried parsley

- Cook pasta in saucepan according to package directions, drain and place on warmed serving platter.

- Heat oil in large frypan and sear half beef strips for about 1 minute. (Beef should be rare.) Season with a little salt and pepper and set aside.

- Sear remaining beef and add to first batch.

- In same frypan, sauté mushrooms and onion just until softened and add to beef.

- In same frypan, stir gravy mix into 1 cup (250 ml) water and mix well. Add white wine, bring to a boil, reduce heat to medium and stir until it thickens.

- Stir in sour cream and parsley and remove from heat. Fold in beef, sauce, onion-mushroom mixture and spoon over warm platter of pasta. Serve 4 to 6.

Stroganoff Made Easy

**455 g (1 pound) beef sirloin, cut
    into (2.5-cm)1-inch squares**
2 tablespoons (30 ml) olive oil
1 onion, chopped
**1 280-g (10-ounce) can cream of
    mushroom soup**
1 tablespoon (15 ml) tomato paste
¼ cup (60 g) sour cream
**340 g (12 ounces) fettuccini
    (medium egg noodles) pasta,
    cooked, drained**

- Sprinkle beef with ample black pepper and place in large frypan with oil. Cook on medium-high heat until beef browns on all sides and stir often. Remove beef with slotted spoon and set aside.

- Reduce heat to medium and sauté onion for about 5 minutes. Stir in soup, tomato paste and ½ cup (125 ml) water; bring to a boil.

- Return beef to frypan, mix well and cook on high just until mixture is thoroughly hot. Stir in sour cream and spoon over hot, cooked pasta. Serves 4.

Beef Stroganoff was invented in Russia in the latter half of the 19th century. While no one knows which chef created it, the name is thought to be in honour of Count Paul Stroganoff. It was common in Russia at that time to name dishes for celebrities.

Spicy Swiss Steak

**680 g (1½ pounds) boneless, beef
round steak**
115 g (4 ounces) spicy bratwurst
2 small onions
**2 tablespoons (35 g) quick-
cooking tapioca (or sago)**
1 teaspoon dried thyme
**2 425-g (15-ounce) cans
stewed tomatoes**
1 teaspoon paprika
**230 g (8 ounces) fettuccini
(medium egg noodles)
pasta, cooked**

- Trim fat from steak and cut into
4 serving-size pieces.

- Brown steak and bratwurst in
frypan. Drain and place in sprayed
4 to 5-L (4 to 5-quart) slow cooker.

- Slice onions and separate
into rings. Cover meat with onions
and sprinkle with tapioca, thyme
and a little salt and pepper. Pour
stewed tomatoes over onion and
seasonings.

- Cover and cook on low for
5 to 8 hours.

- Serve over pasta. Serves 4 to 6.

Classy Beef and Fettuccini

**910 g (2 pounds) lean round steak,
cut in strips**
Olive oil
**2 280-g (10-ounce) cans mushroom
soup**
½ cup (125 ml) cooking sherry
**30 g (1 ounce) onion-mushroom
soup mix**
**340 g (12 ounces) fettuccini
(medium egg noodles) pasta**
¼ cup (60 g) butter

- Preheat oven to 160° C (325° F).

- Brown steak strips in frypan with
a little oil and drain off fat. Stir
in mushroom soup, sherry, onion-
mushroom soup mix and ¾ cup
(175 ml) water. Spoon into
sprayed 3-L (3-quart) baking dish,
cover and bake for 1 hour or until
steak is tender.

- Cook pasta in saucepan according
to package directions, drain and stir
in butter. Spoon onto serving platter
and spoon steak mixture over pasta.
Serves 8 to 10.

Ready Pasta

230 g (8 ounces) fettuccini (medium
  egg noodles) pasta
2 340-g (12-ounce) cans
  corned beef
2 280-g (10-ounce) cans
  cream of celery soup
¾ cup (170 g) mayonnaise
½ cup (125 ml) milk
280 g (10 ounces) frozen green peas,
  thawed
1 roasted red pepper, chopped
¼ cup (40 g) chopped onion
½ cup (60 g) shredded cheddar
  cheese

- Preheat oven to 175° C (350° F).

- Cook pasta in saucepan according to package directions, drain and place in large bowl. Break up corned beef until crumbly.

- Add beef and remaining ingredients, except cheese; mix until they blend well.

- Transfer to sprayed 3-L (3-quart) baking dish; cover and bake for 25 minutes. Uncover and sprinkle cheese over top and return to oven for 5 minutes. Serves 8 to 10.

Pasta needs a lot of water to cook properly. Use at least 2 L (two quarts) for every 230 g (eight ounces) of dried pasta.

Pantry Corned Beef Bake

1 425-g (15-ounce) can corned
    beef, diced
1 cup (115 g) shredded cheddar
    cheese
1 280-g (10-ounce) can cream of
    mushroom soup
1 cup (250 ml) milk
1 small onion, finely chopped
1 red capsicum, seeded, chopped
230 g (8 ounces) pappardelle
    (wide egg noodles) pasta,
    cooked, drained

- Preheat oven to 175° C (350° F).

- Combine corned beef, cheese, mushroom soup, milk, onion, capsicum and a little black pepper in large bowl; mix well. Stir in cooked pasta and mix until all ingredients blend well.

- Spoon into sprayed 3-L (3-quart) baking dish, cover and bake for 45 minutes or until mixture is thoroughly hot. Serves 6.

Pasta
with Chicken

*Chicken is so versatile and when
you add pasta, it's great for
everyday meals – and entertaining.*

Pasta with Chicken Contents

Pasta with Chicken Contents

Naples, Italy, became a centre for mass-producing pasta in the 1800s because its climate was perfect for the drying process. Now, modern equipment makes it possible to make dried pasta anywhere and everywhere and pasta is the most well-known Italian food all around the world.

A Twist on Tetrazzini

3 boneless skinless chicken
   breast halves
1 stick celery, sliced
½ cup (115 g) butter
1 115-g (4-ounce) can sliced
   mushrooms, drained
1 340-g (12-ounce) can evaporated
   milk
230 g (8 ounces) shredded
   processed cheese
230 g (8 ounces) fettuccini
   (medium egg noodles) pasta,
   cooked, drained
⅓ cup (10 g) crushed corn flake
   crumbs

- Preheat oven to 175° C (350° F).

- Boil chicken and celery in large saucepan with boiling, salted water for about 30 minutes. Remove chicken and celery from water and cool. When chicken cools enough, shred and set aside.

- Melt butter in large frypan and add mushrooms and a little salt and pepper. Add evaporated milk and cheese on medium heat; stir until cheese melts. Stir in shredded chicken and bring to a slow boil. Remove from heat.

- Spoon cooked pasta into sprayed 23 x 33-cm (9 x 13-inch) baking dish and spread with back of large spoon. Spoon mushroom-chicken mixture over pasta and stir just slightly, not thoroughly.

- Sprinkle corn flake crumbs over top, cover and bake for 25 minutes. Uncover and cook for additional 10 minutes. Serves 6 to 8.

Alfredo-Chicken Spaghetti

230 g (8 ounces) vermicelli
    (thin spaghetti) pasta,
    broken in thirds
2 teaspoons (10 ml) minced garlic
1 455-g (16-ounce) jar alfredo
    sauce
¼ cup (60 ml) milk
280 g (10 ounces) broccoli
    florets, thawed
2 cups (280 g) cooked, diced
    chicken

- Cook pasta in saucepan according to package directions and drain. Place back in saucepan and stir in garlic, alfredo sauce and milk and mix well.

- Add drained broccoli florets and cook on medium heat for about 5 minutes and stir several times or until broccoli is tender.

- Add more milk if mixture gets too dry. Stir in diced chicken and spoon into serving bowl. Serves 6.

Artichoke-Chicken Pasta

680 g (1½ pounds) boneless chicken
    breast
425 g (15 ounces) artichoke
    hearts, quartered
¾ cup (100 g) roasted red capsicums,
    chopped
460 g (16 ounces) cheddar cheese,
    shredded
1 tablespoon (15 ml) Worcestershire
    sauce
1 280-g (10-ounce) can cream
    of chicken soup
4 cups (300 g) hot, cooked farfalle
    (bow-tie) pasta

- Combine chicken, artichoke, roasted red capsicums, half the cheese, Worcestershire sauce and soup in slow cooker and mix well.

- Cover and cook on low for 6 to 8 hours. About 20 minutes before serving, fold in remaining cheese, hot pasta, and a little salt and pepper. Serves 8.

Bright Broccoli over Fettuccini

230 g (8 ounces) cream
    cheese, cubed
¼ cup (60 g) butter
⅔ cup (210 g) unthickened cream
2 boneless, skinless chicken
    breast halves, cooked, cubed
455 g (16 ounces) frozen chopped
    broccoli florets, thawed
1 red capsicum, seeded, chopped
230 g (8 ounces) fettuccini
    (medium egg noodles) pasta,
    cooked, drained

- Melt cream cheese and butter in large frypan over low heat and stir until smooth.

- Add cream, chicken, broccoli and capsicum; cook, stirring often, over medium heat for 3 minutes. Reduce heat and cook for additional 5 minutes.

- Serve broccoli mixture over cooked pasta. Serves 6 to 8.

Busy Day Chicken Casserole

6 boneless, skinless chicken
    breast halves, cooked
480 g (17 ounces) sour
    cream
200 g (7 ounces) spaghetti
    pasta, broken
2 280-g (10-ounce) cans cream
    of chicken soup
1 115-g (4-ounce) can
    mushrooms, drained
½ cup (115 g) butter,
    melted
1 cup (100 g) grated fresh
    parmesan cheese

- Preheat oven to 175° C (350° F).

- Cut chicken into strips and combine all ingredients, except parmesan cheese with ⅛ teaspoon pepper and mix well.

- Pour into sprayed 23 x 33-cm (9 x 13-inch) baking dish and sprinkle cheese on top. Cover and bake for 50 minutes. Serves 8.

Broccoli-Fusilli in Cream Sauce

455 g (16 ounces) broccoli florets
340 g (12 ounces) fusilli
    (spiral) pasta
½ cup (125 ml) olive oil
4 teaspoons minced garlic
4 boneless, skinless chicken
    breast halves, cut into strips
1 cup (250 ml) cooking white wine
1½ cups (300 ml) chicken stock
230 g (8 ounces) pouring cream
½ cup (60 g) shredded mozzarella
    cheese

- Cook broccoli in boiling water for about 4 minutes or until tender but crisp. Drain and transfer broccoli to large bowl. Add pasta to pot with broccoli water and cook just until tender; drain.

- Heat oil in large frypan and cook garlic and chicken strips for about 5 minutes. Drain and transfer chicken-garlic to bowl with broccoli.

- Stir in wine, stock and cream in frypan and bring to a boil. Reduce heat to medium and cook for 8 minutes, stirring constantly, until sauce thickens slightly.

- Add pasta, broccoli, chicken and cheese to sauce and toss until mixture coats evenly with sauce. Serve immediately. Serves 6.

Rice pasta and brown rice pasta are available for people allergic to gluten (wheat).

Champion Chicken with Chives

455 g (1 pound) boneless, skinless chicken breast halves
1 teaspoon seasoned salt
1 teaspoon lemon pepper
1 tablespoon (15 ml) olive oil
1 onion, chopped
1 red capsicum, chopped
¾ cup (175 ml) milk
2 tablespoons (30 g) butter
145 g (5 ounces) instant pasta and sauce, with sour cream and chives
2 chopped green chillies
2 tablespoons (30 ml) chopped fresh chives

- Cut chicken into thin strips. Season strips with seasoned salt and lemon pepper.

- Heat oil in large frypan over medium-high heat and cook chicken strips, capsicum and onions for about 5 minutes or until chicken is no longer pink. Remove from frypan and set aside.

- In same frypan, bring 1¼ cups (310 ml) water, milk and butter to a boil. Reduce heat to medium, cook pasta and seasoning sachet for about 10 minutes and stir often.

- Stir in chicken strips and green chillies, spoon into serving bowl and sprinkle with chopped chives. Let stand for 5 minutes before serving. Serves 4.

Cheesy Fettuccini and Chicken

255 g (9 ounces) refrigerated fettuccini (medium egg noodles) pasta

2 cups (140 g) small fresh broccoli florets

⅓ cup (75 ml) Italian salad dressing

455 g (1 pound) chicken breast strips for stir-fry

½ red onion, cut into wedges

1 roasted red capsicum, sliced

145 g (5 ounces) grated parmesan cheese

- Cook pasta with broccoli florets according to package directions on pasta. Drain and toss with 2 tablespoons (30 ml) salad dressing. Cover and keep warm.

- Spray large frypan and heat over medium-high heat. Add chicken strips, onion and a little salt and pepper. Cook for about 5 minutes, stirring often until chicken is no longer pink in centre.

- Stir in capsicum and remaining salad dressing and cook for about 3 minutes, stirring often until mixture is warm. Serve chicken mixture over pasta and broccoli. Sprinkle with parmesan cheese when ready to serve. Serves 8.

Cheesy, Cheesy Chicken

Cheese lovers dig in!
This is a real winner!

1 onion, chopped
1 red and ½ green capsicum,
    seeded, chopped
½ cup (115 g) butter
1 280-g (10-ounce) can
    cream of chicken soup
1 115-g (4-ounce) can
    sliced mushrooms
½ teaspoon dried coriander
½ teaspoon dried basil
1 teaspoon celery salt
½ teaspoon garlic pepper
230 g (8 ounces) fettuccini
    (medium egg noodles) pasta,
    cooked al dente, drained
4–5 boneless, skinless
    chicken breast halves,
    cooked, cubed
425 g (15 ounces) ricotta cheese

455 g (16 ounces) shredded cheddar
    cheese
⅓ cup (35 g) grated parmesan
    cheese
1 cup (60 g) breadcrumbs

- Preheat oven to 175° C (350° F).

- Sauté onion and capsicums with
  5 tablespoons (75 g) butter in
  frypan. Remove from heat and stir
  in soup, mushrooms, coriander,
  basil, celery salt, garlic pepper and
  a little salt.

- Combine pasta, chicken, cheeses
  and soup-mushroom mixture in
  large bowl. Mix well.

- Spoon into sprayed 23 x 33-cm
  (9 x 13-inch) baking dish.

- Melt 3 tablespoons (45 g) butter
  and combine with breadcrumbs.
  Sprinkle over casserole.

- Cover and bake for 45 minutes.
  Serves 8.

Chicken Alfredo

680 g (1½ pounds) boneless chicken
   thighs
2 sticks celery, sliced diagonally
1 red capsicum, seeded,
   julienned
1 455-g (16-ounce) jar alfredo
   sauce
3 cups (215 g) fresh broccoli florets
230 g (8 ounces) linguine
   (thin egg noodles) pasta
145 g (5 ounces) grated parmesan
   cheese

- Cut chicken into strips. Layer chicken, celery and capsicum in 4 to 5-L (4 to 5-quart) slow cooker. Pour alfredo sauce evenly over vegetables. Cover and cook on low for 5 to 6 hours.

- About 30 minutes before serving, turn heat to high and add broccoli florets to chicken-alfredo mixture. Cover and cook for additional 30 minutes.

- Cook pasta according to package directions and drain. Just before serving pour pasta into cooker, mix and sprinkle parmesan cheese on top. Serves 8.

Chicken and Noodles

910 g (2 pounds) boneless, skinless
   chicken breast halves
¼ cup (30 g) cornflour
⅓ cup (75 ml) soy sauce
2 onions, chopped
3 sticks celery, sliced diagonally
1 red capsicum, seeded,
   julienned
2 400-g (14-ounce) cans mixed
   Chinese vegetables, drained
¼ cup (60 ml) treacle
2 cups (110 g) chow mein noodles,
   cooked

- Place chicken breasts and 2 cups (500 ml) water in sprayed slow cooker. Cover and cook on low for 3 to 4 hours. At least 1 hour before serving, remove chicken and cut into bite-size pieces.

- Combine cornflour and soy sauce in bowl and mix well. Stir into slow cooker. Add onions, celery, capsicum, mixed vegetables and treacle. Turn heat to high and cook for 1 to 2 hours.

- Serve over noodles. Serves 4 to 6.

Chicken and Pasta

455 g (16 ounces) frozen
    whole green beans, thawed
1 onion, chopped
1 cup (70 g) fresh mushroom
    halves
3 boneless, skinless
    chicken breast halves
1 425-g (15-ounce) can Italian
    stewed tomatoes
1 chicken stock cube
1 teaspoon minced garlic
1 teaspoon Italian seasoning
230 g (8 ounces) fettuccini (medium
    egg noodles) pasta
115 g (4 ounces) grated parmesan
    cheese

- Place green beans, onion and mushrooms in sprayed 4-L (4-quart) slow cooker.
- Cut chicken into 2.5-cm (1-inch) pieces and place over vegetables.
- Combine stewed tomatoes, chicken stock cube, garlic and Italian seasoning in small bowl. Pour over chicken.
- Cover and cook on low for 5 to 6 hours.
- Cook pasta according to package directions and drain.
- Serve chicken over pasta sprinkled with parmesan cheese. Serves 4.

TIP: Add ¼ cup (60 g) butter to give this dish a richer taste.

Chicken and Spaghetti

How could anything be easier?

4 boneless, skinless chicken
    breast halves, cooked,
    cubed
230 g (8 ounces) sour cream
200 g (7 ounces) spaghetti pasta,
    broken
2 280-g (10-ounce) cans cream
    of chicken soup
1 115-g (4-ounce) can
    mushrooms, drained
½ cup (115 g) butter, melted
1 cup (100 g) grated parmesan
    cheese

- Preheat oven to 160° C (325° F).

- Combine chicken, sour cream, pasta, chicken soup, mushrooms, butter and ¼ teaspoon (1 ml) pepper in large bowl.

- Pour into sprayed 23 x 33-cm (9 x 13-inch) baking dish.

- Sprinkle cheese on top of casserole.

- Cover and bake for 50 minutes. Serves 8.

There is a legend that Marco Polo, the explorer from Venice, brought pasta to Italy from China in the 13th century. But pasta existed in Italy even before Rome was founded.

Chicken and Spinach Fettuccini

230 g (8 ounces) spinach fettuccini (medium egg noodles) pasta
1 170-g (6-ounce) jar marinated artichoke hearts
1 small onion, finely chopped
1 red capsicum, seeded, chopped
1 cup (310 g) unthickened cream
⅔ cup (70 g) grated parmesan cheese
2½ cups (350 g) cooked, cubed chicken breasts

- Cook pasta according to package directions; drain and keep warm.

- Cut artichokes in half; drain and set aside 2 tablespoons (30 ml) marinade. Heat marinade to boiling in large frypan and add onion and capsicum. Cook for about 5 minutes, stirring often or until tender but crisp.

- Stir cream into onion-capsicum mixture and heat, but don't boil.

- Stir in artichoke hearts, cheese and chicken and mix until blended well. Add pasta and toss. Sprinkle with black pepper. Serves 8.

Dried pasta is called pasta secca *in Italy;*
fresh pasta is called pasta fresca.

Chicken and Vegetables

85 g (3 ounces) chicken-flavoured
    instant ramen noodles
455 g (16 ounces) frozen broccoli
    florets, cauliflower and carrots
⅔ cup (150 ml) sweet-and-sour
    sauce
3 boneless, skinless chicken
    breast halves, cooked,
    cut into thin strips

- Reserve seasoning packet from
  noodles. Cook noodles and
  vegetables in 2 cups (500 ml)
  boiling water in saucepan for
  3 minutes, stirring occasionally,
  and drain.

- Combine noodle-vegetable mixture
  with seasoning packet, sweet-and-
  sour sauce and a little salt and
  pepper. (You may want to add
  1 tablespoon/15 ml soy sauce.)

- Add chicken and heat thoroughly.
  Serves 8.

Chicken Delight

5–6 boneless, skinless
    chicken breast halves
1 teaspoon chicken seasoning
1 280-g (10-ounce) can cream
    of chicken soup
1 280-g (10-ounce) can cream of
    asparagus soup
½ cup (125 ml) white cooking wine
340 g (12 ounces) fettuccini (medium
    egg noodles) pasta, cooked

- Cut chicken breasts in half if they
  are particularly large. Place breast
  halves, sprinkled with pepper and
  chicken seasoning in sprayed
  slow cooker.

- Combine soups and wine in
  saucepan and heat enough to mix
  well. Pour over chicken. Cover and
  cook on low for 5 to 6 hours. Serve
  chicken and sauce over hot, cooked
  pasta. Serves 8 to 10.

Chicken Chow Mein

3½ cups (490 g) cooked, cubed
  chicken breasts
2 280-g (10-ounce) cans cream
  of chicken soup
2 425-g (15-ounce) cans Chinese
  mixed vegetables, drained
1 230-g (8-ounce) can sliced
  water chestnuts, drained
¾ cup (100 g) chopped cashews
1 green capsicum,
  seeded, chopped
1 onion, chopped
1 cup (100 g) chopped celery
¼ teaspoon hot chilli sauce
1¼ cups (125 g) chow mein
  noodles

- Preheat oven to 175° C (350° F).

- Combine chicken, soup, vegetables, water chestnuts, cashew nuts, capsicum, onion, celery and hot chilli sauce in large bowl. Stir to mix well.

- Spoon into sprayed 23 x 33-cm (9 x 13-inch) baking dish. Sprinkle chow mein noodles over top of casserole.

- Bake for 35 minutes or until it bubbles at edges of casserole. Let stand for 5 minutes before serving. Serves 8.

*Because pasta has such a long shelf life, it was often
used for ocean voyages in the days of sailing ships.*

Chicken Dish, WOW!

1 280-g (10-ounce) can cream
    of chicken soup
1 280-g (10-ounce) can cream of
    celery sauce
1 145-g (5-ounce) can
    evaporated milk
2 425-g (15-ounce) cans French-
    style green beans, drained
1 chicken stock cube
4 cups (560 g) cooked, cubed
    chicken breasts
1 red capsicum, chopped
2 sticks celery, sliced
¼ cup (40 g) chopped onion
1 cup (55 g) chow mein noodles
½ cup (85 g) slivered almonds
85 g (3 ounces) fried
    onion rings

- Preheat oven to 175° C (350° F).

- Combine soups and evaporated milk and mix well.

- Fold in green beans, chicken stock cube, chicken, capsicum, celery, onion, noodles, almonds, and ½ teaspoon each of salt and pepper.

- Spoon into sprayed 23 x 33-cm (9 x 13-inch) baking dish.

- Cover and bake for 35 minutes. Remove from oven and sprinkle onion rings over casserole.

- Place back in oven and bake for additional 10 minutes. Serves 8 to 10.

TIP: *This casserole may easily be made ahead of time and baked the next day. Just wait to add the onion rings until called for.*

Chicken Elegant

This is rich, but worth the calories!

3 tablespoons (75 g) butter
3 tablespoons (45 g) flour
1¾ cups (425 ml) milk
½ cup (115 g) shredded sharp
    cheddar cheese
½ cup (110 g) shredded Swiss
    cheese
½ teaspoon (2 ml) Worcestershire
    sauce
1 cup (140 g) cooked, diced chicken
1 cup (140 g) cooked, diced ham
1 115-g (4-ounce) can sliced
    mushrooms, drained
1 roasted red capsicum, chopped
Fettuccini (medium egg
    noodles) pasta, cooked

- Melt butter in saucepan and blend
  in flour. Add milk all at once, cook
  and stir until sauce is thick and
  bubbly. Remove from heat, add
  cheeses and stir until they melt.

- Stir in Worcestershire sauce,
  chicken or turkey, ham, mushrooms
  and roasted red capsicum. Heat
  thoroughly and serve over pasta.
  Serves 6 to 8.

Chicken Dinner

5 boneless, skinless chicken
    breast halves
1 455-g (16-ounce) jar alfredo
    sauce
455 g (16 ounces) frozen
    green peas, thawed
1½ cups (175 g) shredded
    mozzarella cheese
230 g (8 ounces) pappardelle (wide
    egg noodles) pasta, cooked
2 tablespoons (30 g) butter

- Cut chicken into strips and place in
  sprayed slow cooker.

- Combine alfredo sauce, peas and
  cheese in bowl and mix well.
  Spoon over chicken strips.

- Cover and cook on low for
  5 to 6 hours.

- When ready to serve, spoon over
  hot, cooked pasta with butter.
  Serves 4 to 5.

Chicken Lasagna

1 455-g (16-ounce) jar alfredo
    sauce
1 roasted red capsicum, diced
⅓ cup (75 ml) cooking white wine
280 g (10 ounces) frozen
    chopped spinach, thawed
425 g (15 ounces) ricotta cheese
½ cup (50 g) grated parmesan cheese
1 egg, beaten
8 lasagna sheets
3 cups (420 g) cooked, shredded
    chicken
340 g (12 ounces) shredded cheddar
    cheese

- Preheat oven to 175° C (350° F).

- Combine alfredo sauce, roasted red capsicum and wine in large bowl; reserve ½ cup (125 ml) for top of lasagna.

- Squeeze spinach between paper towels to completely remove excess moisture. In separate bowl, combine spinach, ricotta, parmesan cheese and egg. Mix well.

- Place 4 lasagna sheets in sprayed 23 x 33-cm (9 x 13-inch) baking dish. Layer with half remaining sauce, half spinach-ricotta mixture and half chicken. (Spinach-ricotta mixture will be fairly dry so you will need to 'spoon' it on and spread out.)

- Sprinkle with half cheese. For last layer, place lasagna sheets, remaining sauce, remaining spinach-ricotta mixture, remaining chicken and reserved sauce on top.

- Cover and bake for 45 minutes. Uncover and sprinkle remaining cheese over top and return to oven for 6 minutes. Let lasagna stand for 10 minutes before serving. Serves 10 to 12.

Chicken Linguine

455 g (1 pound) boneless, skinless chicken breast halves, cut into strips
Olive oil
1 795-g (28-ounce) can spaghetti sauce
455 g (16 ounces) frozen broccoli florets, carrots and cauliflower, thawed
1 capsicum, seeded, chopped
⅓ cup (30 g) grated parmesan cheese
340 g (12 ounces) linguine (thin egg noodles) pasta, cooked, drained

- Cook half chicken strips with a little oil in large frypan over medium heat until light brown. Remove and set aside. Repeat with remaining chicken and set aside.

- In same frypan combine spaghetti sauce, garlic, onion, vegetables and cheese and bring to a boil. Reduce heat to medium-low, cover and cook for 10 minutes or until vegetables are tender. Stir occasionally.

- Return chicken to frypan and heat thoroughly.

- Place cooked pasta on serving platter and spoon chicken mixture over pasta. Serves 12.

TIP: *Break linguine into thirds before cooking to make serving a little easier.*

Linguine, like most pastas, gets its name from its shape; the word means 'little tongues'.

Chicken Meets Italy

**455 g (16 ounces) frozen
  whole green beans, thawed
1 onion, chopped
1 cup (70 g) halved fresh
  mushrooms
3 boneless, skinless chicken
  breast halves
1 425-g (15-ounce) can Italian
  stewed tomatoes
1 chicken stock cube
1 teaspoon minced garlic
1 teaspoon Italian seasoning
230 g (8 ounces) fettuccini (medium
  egg noodles) pasta
145 g (4 ounces) parmesan cheese**

- Place green beans, onion and mushrooms in sprayed 4 to 5-L (4 to 5-quart) slow cooker. Cut chicken into 2.5-cm (1-inch) pieces and place over vegetables.

- Combine stewed tomatoes, chicken stock cube, garlic and Italian seasoning in small bowl. Pour over chicken. Cover and cook on low for 5 to 6 hours.

- Cook pasta according to package directions and drain. Serve chicken over pasta and sprinkle with parmesan cheese. Serves 8.

TIP: For added flavour, you can add ¼ cup (60 g) butter.

Chicken Parmesan and Spaghetti

400 g (14 ounces) frozen, cooked,
  breaded chicken cutlets,
  thawed
1 795-g (28-ounce) jar spaghetti
  sauce
290 g (10 ounces) grated parmesan
  cheese
230 g (8 ounces) vermicelli (thin
  spaghetti) pasta, cooked

- Preheat oven to 190° C (375° F).

- Place cutlets in sprayed
  23 x 33-cm (9 x 13-inch) baking
  dish and top each with about
  ¼ cup (60 ml) spaghetti sauce
  and 1 heaped tablespoon (15 ml)
  parmesan. Bake for 15 minutes.

- Place cooked pasta on serving
  platter and top with cutlets.
  Sprinkle remaining cheese over
  cutlets. Heat remaining spaghetti
  sauce and serve with chicken and
  pasta. Serves 6 to 8.

Chicken Spaghetti

3 boneless, skinless chicken
  breasts, boiled
1 280-g (10-ounce) can tomatoes
2 green chillies, chopped
1 280-g (10-ounce) can cream
  of mushroom soup
460 g (16 ounces) shredded cheddar
  cheese
1 340-g (12-ounce) package
  spaghetti pasta

- Preheat oven to 175° C (350° F).

- Shred cooked chicken into large
  bowl. Add tomatoes, soup and
  cheddar cheese. Boil pasta in
  saucepan according to package
  directions and drain.

- Add to chicken mixture and mix
  well. Pour into 3-L (3-quart) baking
  dish. Cover and bake for
  35 minutes. Serves 6.

Chicken Tarragon

*Tarragon works wonders
for this chicken.*

**230 g (8 ounces) fettuccini (medium
egg noodles) pasta
1 cup (250 ml) dry white wine
1 teaspoon (5 ml) dried tarragon
leaves
30 g (1 ounce) instant
vegetable soup mix
4 boneless, skinless chicken
breast halves
230 g (8 ounces) sour cream**

- Cook pasta in saucepan according to package directions, drain and set aside. Pour 2 cups (500 ml) water into large frypan. Over medium heat add wine and tarragon and bring to boil. Stir in dry soup mix and boil 5 minutes.

- Add chicken and reduce heat. Cover and simmer for 15 minutes. Arrange pasta on serving dish. Use slotted spoon to remove chicken, place on top of pasta and cover with foil.

- Boil juices in frypan for about 5 to 10 minutes or until liquid reduces to ½ cup (125 ml). Turn heat to low and stir constantly while adding sour cream. Heat 3 to 4 minutes more and pour over chicken. Serves 6.

*It is better to measure dried pasta by weight
(grams/ounces) rather than by volume (cups/millilitres).*

Chicken with Mushrooms and Capsicums

455 g (16 ounces) fresh mushrooms, sliced, divided
2 red capsicums, seeded, chopped
1½ cups (90 g) seasoned breadcrumbs
6 boneless, skinless chicken breast halves
2 eggs, beaten
2 tablespoons (30 ml) butter
6 slices Swiss cheese
1 cup (250 ml) chicken stock
340 g (12 ounces) fettuccini (medium egg noodles) pasta
2 tablespoons (30 g) butter

- Preheat oven to 175° C (350° F).

- Place half mushrooms and half capsicums into sprayed 23 x 33-cm (9 x 13-inch) baking dish.

- Place breadcrumbs in shallow bowl. Dip each chicken breast in beaten eggs and dredge in breadcrumbs.

- Melt butter in large frypan, brown both sides of chicken and place chicken on top of mushroom-pepper mixture in baking dish. Arrange remaining mushroom-pepper mixture over chicken breasts.

- Place cheese slices over chicken and pour stock in baking dish. Cover and bake for 35 minutes.

- Cook pasta according to package directions, drain and add butter. Stir until butter melts and place noodles on serving platter.

- Arrange chicken, mushrooms and capsicums over pasta and serve hot. Serves 6.

Chicken-Broccoli Casserole

8 boneless, skinless chicken
   breast halves, sliced
½ cup (115 g) butter
½ cup (60 g) flour
2 cups (625 g) unthickened
   cream
½ litre (14 ounces) chicken
   stock
230 g (8 ounces) shredded cheddar
   cheese
145 g (5 ounces) fresh grated
   parmesan cheese
2 tablespoons (30 ml) lemon juice
1 tablespoon (15 ml) mustard
2 tablespoons (10 g) dried
   parsley
1 tablespoon (15 g) dried onion
   flakes or 3 tablespoons (30 g)
   fresh chopped onion
¾ cup (170 g) mayonnaise
2 280-g (10-ounce) packets frozen
   broccoli florets,
   slightly cooked
200 g (7 ounces) vermicelli (thin
   spaghetti) pasta

- Preheat oven to 175° C (350° F).

- Wash chicken and dry well with paper towels. Melt butter in large saucepan or roasting pan and add flour.

- Add cream and stir constantly over medium-low heat until thick. Add chicken stock, half cheddar cheese, parmesan cheese, lemon juice, ¼ teaspoon pepper, mustard, parsley, onion and 2 teaspoons (10 ml) salt.

- Heat on low until cheeses melt. Remove from heat and add mayonnaise. Add broccoli and chicken slices to sauce.

- Cook pasta according to package directions. Drain and pour into 25 x 38-cm (10 x 15-inch) glass dish. (This will not fit in 23 x 33-cm/9 x 13-inch glass dish.)

- Spread sauce and chicken mixture over pasta and sprinkle remaining cheese over top. Cook for 40 minutes. Serves 8 to 10.

Chicken-Ham Lasagna

1 115-g (4-ounce) can chopped
  mushrooms, drained
1 large onion, chopped
¼ cup (60 g) butter
½ cup (60 g) flour
Ground nutmeg
½ litre (14 ounces) chicken
  stock
500 ml (1 pint) unthickened cream
85 g (3 ounces) grated parmesan
  cheese
455 g (16 ounces) frozen
  broccoli florets
9 lasagna sheets, cooked, drained
1½ cups (210 g) cooked, finely diced
  ham
340 g (12 ounces) shredded Colby
  cheese
2 cups (280 g) cooked, shredded
  chicken breasts

- Preheat oven to 175° C (350° F).

- Sauté mushrooms and onion in
  butter in large frypan. Stir in flour,
  1 teaspoon salt and ¼ teaspoon
  pepper and a dash of nutmeg and
  stir until they blend well.

- Gradually stir in stock and cream,
  cook and stir for about 2 minutes or
  until it thickens. Stir in parmesan
  cheese.

- Cut broccoli florets into smaller
  pieces and discard stems. Add to
  cream mixture.

- Spread about ½ cup (125 ml)
  cream-broccoli mixture in sprayed
  25 x 38-cm (10 x 15-inch) baking
  dish. Layer with 3 lasagna sheets,
  one-third of remaining broccoli
  mixture, ½ cup (120 ml) ham, 1 cup
  (240 ml) chicken and 1 cup
  (240 ml) Colby cheese.

- Top with 3 more lasagna sheets,
  one-third of broccoli mixture, 1 cup
  (240 ml) ham, 1 cup (240 ml)
  chicken and 1 cup (120 ml) Colby
  cheese. Add remaining lasagna
  sheets, chicken and cream-broccoli
  mixture.

- Cover and bake for 50 minutes
  or until it bubbles. Sprinkle with
  remaining cheese. Let stand for
  15 minutes before cutting into
  squares to serve. Serves 8 to 10.

Chicken-Pasta Delight

This recipe is a hearty main dish and the capsicums make it colourful as well. It's a great family dinner.

2 sticks celery, chopped
½ onion, chopped
½ green capsicum, seeded, chopped
½ red capsicum, seeded, chopped
6 tablespoons (90 g) butter
3 cups (420 g) cooked, cubed chicken breasts
1 115-g (4-ounce) can sliced mushrooms, drained
1 455-g (16-ounce) jar sun-dried tomato pasta sauce
½ cup (155 g) unthickened cream
2 chicken stock cubes
230 g (8 ounces) fettuccini (medium egg noodles) pasta, cooked, drained
1 cup (30 g) cornflake crumbs
½ cup (60 g) shredded cheddar cheese

- Preheat oven to 160° C (325° F).

- Combine celery, onion, capsicums and 4 tablespoons (60 g) butter in frypan or large saucepan and sauté for about 5 minutes.

- Remove from heat and add chicken, mushrooms, pasta sauce, cream, chicken stock cubes and pasta and mix well. Pour into sprayed 3-L (3-quart) baking dish.

- For topping combine cornflakes and cheese into a bowl and sprinkle over casserole. Bake for 20 minutes or until casserole bubbles around edges. Serves 6.

Chicken-Orzo Florentine

4 boneless, skinless chicken
    breast halves
¾ cup (130 g) orzo (tiny) pasta
230 g (8 ounces) fresh mushrooms,
    sliced
280 g (10 ounces) frozen
    spinach, thawed,
    drained
1 280-g (10-ounce) can
    mushroom soup
½ cup (110 g) mayonnaise
1 tablespoon (15 ml) lemon juice
230 g (8 ounces) shredded Colby
    cheese
½ cup (60 g) seasoned breadcrumbs
1 teaspoon dried basil

- Preheat oven to 175° C (350° F).

- Cook chicken in boiling water for about 15 minutes and reserve stock. Cut chicken in bite-size pieces and set aside. Pour stock through strainer and cook pasta in remaining stock.

- Sauté mushrooms in large, sprayed frypan until tender. Remove from heat and stir in chicken, pasta, spinach, soup, mayonnaise, lemon juice and ½ teaspoon pepper. Fold in half cheese and mix well.

- Spoon into sprayed 23 x 33-cm (9 x 13-inch) baking dish and sprinkle with remaining cheese, basil and breadcrumbs. Bake for 35 minutes. Serves 6.

Chicken-Orzo Dinner

145 g (5 ounces) orzo (tiny)
    pasta
2 chicken stock cubes
200 g (7 ounces) chicken cooked,
    and cut into strips
280 g (10 ounces) frozen corn kernels
280 g (10 ounces) frozen cut green
    beans
¼ cup (60 ml) extra-virgin olive oil
1 teaspoon minced garlic

- Cook pasta with stock cubes in saucepan according to package directions. Add chicken strips, corn, green beans, olive oil, garlic, ¼ cup (60 ml) water and a little salt and pepper and mix well.

- Cook on low heat and stir several times until mixture is hot, for about 10 to 15 minutes. Serves 6.

Creamy Chicken Pasta

280 g (10 ounces)
    penne (tube) pasta
1 tablespoon (15 ml) olive oil
1 (12-ounce) serve roasted
    chicken meat, shredded
2 tablespoons (30 g) pesto
¾ cup (60 g) pouring cream

- Cook pasta in large saucepan according to package directions. Drain and place back in saucepan. Gently stir in oil, chicken, pesto and cream.

- Place saucepan over low heat, simmer just until cream is absorbed. Spoon into serving bowl and serve immediately. Serves 6.

Chicken-Pasta Dinner Supreme

280 g (10 ounces) capelli d'angelo (angel hair) pasta
1 onion, chopped
1 red capsicum, seeded, chopped
2 teaspoons minced garlic
Olive oil
280 g (10 ounces) fresh baby spinach
2 tomatoes, chopped, drained
3 cups (420 g) cooked, chopped chicken breasts
2 tablespoons (30 ml), cooked, crumbled bacon
115 g (4 ounces) creamy Italian salad dressing
¼ cup (35 g) crumbled feta cheese

- Cook pasta in saucepan according to package directions. Drain and set aside.

- Sauté onion, capsicum and garlic in large frypan with a little oil. Add spinach and ¼ cup (60 ml) water. Cover and cook for 3 minutes or until spinach wilts.

- Stir in tomatoes, chicken, bacon and salad dressing and cook until mixture heats thoroughly.

- Place pasta on serving platter and spoon chicken mixture over pasta. Sprinkle with feta cheese. Serves 8.

TIP: *Leftover chicken or deli turkey may be substituted for chicken breasts.*

Chicken-Spaghetti Bake

280 g (10 ounces) spaghetti pasta
1 onion, chopped
1 stick celery, chopped
1 capsicum, seeded,
chopped
Olive oil
1 425-g (15-ounce) can
stewed tomatoes
1 teaspoon paprika
1 115-g (4-ounce) can chopped
mushrooms, drained
1 teaspoon minced garlic
½ cup (125 ml) chicken stock
4 cups (560 g) cooked, cubed
chicken
340 g (12 ounces) shredded
processed cheese

- Preheat oven to 175° C (350° F).

- Cook pasta in saucepan according to package directions.

- Sauté onion, celery and capsicum in saucepan with a little oil. Add tomatoes, paprika, mushrooms, garlic, stock, chicken and a little salt and pepper.

- Stir in cheese and spoon into sprayed 4-L (4-quart) baking dish.

- Cover and bake for 45 minutes. Serves 8.

Pasta can be easily reheated in a microwave oven. Usually 1 to 3 minutes on high will work, and toss the pasta halfway through the cooking time. You can also put the pasta in a colander and pour very hot water over it.

Chicken-Spinach Lasagna

9 lasagna sheets
½ cup (115 g) butter
1 teaspoon minced garlic
½ cup (60 g) flour
½ litre (14 ounces) chicken
    stock
1½ cups (465 g) unthickened
    cream
455 g (16 ounces) shredded
    mozzarella cheese
1½ teaspoons oregano
425 g (15 ounces) ricotta
    cheese
2 cups (280 g) cooked, shredded
    chicken
455 g (16 ounces) frozen chopped
    spinach, thawed, drained
¼ cup (25 g) grated parmesan
    cheese

- Preheat oven to 175° C (350° F).

- Cook lasagna sheets in saucepan according to package directions; drain and rinse with cold water. Place lasagna sheets (not touching) on sheet of baking paper.

- Melt butter in large saucepan on medium heat, add garlic and flour and stir until bubbly. Mix in stock and cream, bring to a boil and stir constantly for 1 minute.

- Stir in half mozzarella and season with oregano, 1 teaspoon (15 ml) black pepper and a little salt. Remove from heat and set aside.

- Spread one-third stock-cream mixture in sprayed 23 x 33-cm (9 x 13-inch) baking pan. Layer with one-third lasagna sheets, ricotta, spinach and chicken.

- Place one-third lasagna sheets over chicken and layer stock-cream mixture, spinach and remaining mozzarella cheese.

- Arrange remaining 3 lasagna sheets over cheese and spread remaining stock-cream mixture evenly over noodles. Sprinkle with parmesan cheese and bake for 35 minutes. Let stand for 10 minutes before serving. Serves 10 to 12.

Chinese Chicken

3½ cups (490 g) cooked, cubed
    chicken
2 280-g (10-ounce) cans cream
    of chicken soup
1 455-g (16-ounce) can Chinese
    mixed vegetables,
    drained
1 230-g (8-ounce) can sliced
    water chestnuts,
    drained
¾ cup (100 g) cashew nuts
1 cup (150 g) chopped green
    capsicum
1 bunch spring onions
    with tops, sliced
½ cup (50 g) chopped celery
⅓ teaspoon hot chilli sauce
¼ teaspoon curry powder
1 145-g (5-ounce) can chow
    mein noodles

- Preheat oven to 175° C (350° F).

- Combine chicken, soups,
  vegetables, water chestnuts, cashew
  nuts, capsicum, spring onions,
  celery, hot chilli sauce and curry
  powder in large bowl. Stir to
  mix well.

- Spoon mixture into sprayed
  23 x 33-cm (9 x 13-inch) glass
  baking dish and sprinkle noodles
  over casserole.

- Bake for 30 to 35 minutes or until
  bubbly at edges. Set aside for about
  5 minutes before serving. Serves 6.

Italians eat about 60 pounds of pasta per person every year.

Chinese Garden

The combination of ingredients in this recipe makes a great-tasting casserole.

170 g (6 ounces) fried rice with
    oriental seasoning
1 teaspoon slivered almonds, finely
    chopped
2 tablespoons (30 g) butter
1 onion, chopped
2 cups (200 g) chopped celery
1 425-g (15-ounce) can Chinese
    vegetables, drained
1 230-g (8-ounce) can sliced
    bamboo shoots
3½ cups (490 g) cooked, chopped
    chicken
1 280-g (10-ounce) can cream
    of chicken soup
1 cup (225 g) mayonnaise
2 tablespoons (30 ml) soy sauce
½ teaspoon garlic powder
1 cup (55 g) chow mein noodles

- Preheat oven to 175° C (350° F).

- Cook rice in saucepan according to package directions and set aside.

- Heat butter in large frypan and sauté onion and celery. Add Chinese vegetables, bamboo shoots and chicken and mix well.

- Heat chicken soup, mayonnaise, soy sauce, garlic powder and a little pepper in saucepan just enough to mix well.

- Combine rice, vegetable-chicken mixture and soup mixture with almonds in large bowl and mix well. Transfer to sprayed 3-L (3-quart) baking dish.

- Sprinkle noodles over casserole. Bake for 35 minutes. Serves 6 to 8.

Creamy Chicken Bake

230 g (8 ounces) fettuccini (medium
   egg noodles) pasta
455 g (16 ounces) frozen broccoli
   florets, thawed, trimmed
¼ cup (60 g) butter,
   melted
230 g (8 ounces) shredded cheddar
   cheese
1 280-g (10-ounce) can cream
   of chicken soup
1 cup (310 g) unthickened cream
¼ teaspoon ground mustard
3 cups (420 g) cooked, cubed
   chicken breasts
⅔ cup (110 g) slivered almonds

- Preheat oven to 160° C (325° F).

- Cook pasta in saucepan according to package directions, drain and keep warm.

- Combine pasta and broccoli in large bowl. Add butter and cheese and stir until cheese melts.

- Stir in chicken soup, cream, mustard, chicken and 1 teaspoon each of salt and pepper. Spoon into sprayed 3-L (3-quart) baking dish.

- Cover and bake for about 25 minutes. Remove from oven, sprinkle with slivered almonds and cook for additional 15 minutes. Serves 6.

Creamy Lemon Fettuccini

340 g (12 ounces) fettuccini (medium egg noodles) pasta
2 bunches fresh asparagus, trimmed
3 tablespoons (45 ml) olive oil
2 cups (280 g) bite-size chunks roast chicken
¾ cup (100 g) coarsely chopped walnuts
1 455-g (16-ounce) jar alfredo sauce
⅓ cup (75 ml) lemon juice
½ cup (60 g) shredded mozzarella cheese

- Preheat oven to 190° C (375° F).

- Cook pasta in saucepan according to package directions, drain and return to pot, covered to keep warm. Cut asparagus into 5-cm (2-inch) pieces. Place asparagus in single layer in sprayed 23 x 33-cm (9 x 13-inch) baking dish and drizzle with oil; roast for 10 minutes.

- Add chicken, walnuts and a little salt and pepper and stir to blend well. Cook for an additional 5 minutes to toast walnuts lightly and stir often. Transfer pasta to serving bowl and spoon asparagus mixture over pasta. Toss to blend well.

- Pour alfredo sauce into microwave-safe bowl and heat on full power just until sauce begins to boil. Stir in lemon juice and pour over fettuccini-asparagus mixture. Toss well. Sprinkle with mozzarella cheese and serve immediately. Serves 6 to 8.

Delicious Chicken Pasta

455 g (1 pound) chicken pieces
Lemon-herb seasoning
3 tablespoons (45 ml) butter
1 onion, coarsely chopped
1 425-g (15-ounce) can diced
    tomatoes
1 280-g (10-ounce) can
    mushroom soup
230 g (8 ounces) capelli
    d'angelo (angel hair)
    pasta

- Pat chicken pieces dry with several paper towels and sprinkle ample amount of seasoning. Melt butter in large frypan, brown chicken and place in oval slow cooker. Pour remaining butter from frypan over chicken and cover with onion.

- In separate bowl, combine tomatoes and mushroom soup and pour over chicken and onions. Cover and cook on low for 4 to 5 hours.

- When ready to serve, cook pasta in saucepan according to package directions. Serve chicken and sauce over pasta. Serves 8.

Family-Night Spaghetti

6 frozen crumbed,
    chicken breast halves
230 g (8 ounces) spaghetti pasta
1 510-g (18-ounces) jar spaghetti
    sauce
740 g (26 ounces) shredded
    mozzarella cheese

- Bake chicken breasts according to package directions and keep warm. Cook pasta in saucepan according to package directions, drain and arrange on platter.

- Place spaghetti sauce in saucepan with 1 cup (115 g) mozzarella cheese and heat slightly, but do not boil.

- Spoon about half sauce over pasta and arrange chicken breasts over top. Spoon remaining spaghetti sauce on chicken and sprinkle remaining cheese over top. Serves 6.

Dijon-Tarragon Chicken

230 g (8 ounces) fettuccini (medium
   egg noodles) pasta
1 teaspoon (5 ml) seasoned salt
2 tablespoons (30 g) butter
455 g (1 pound) boneless skinless
   chicken breasts, cut
   into 1.2-cm (½-inch) pieces
230 g (8 ounces) sour
   cream
2 tablespoons (30 g) Dijon-style
   mustard
1 teaspoon dried tarragon
   leaves
½ cup (70 g) frozen green peas,
   thawed
2 tablespoons (10 g) chopped fresh
   parsley

- Cook pasta according to package directions, drain and cover to keep warm.

- Sprinkle seasoned salt over chicken. Melt butter in large frypan on medium-high heat. Cook chicken for 10 minutes, stirring frequently until centre is no longer pink.

- Combine sour cream, mustard and tarragon leaves in small bowl, mix until smooth.

- Pour into frypan with chicken and add green peas. Cook for about 5 minutes, stirring frequently. Serve chicken mixture over pasta and sprinkle with parsley. Serves 6 to 8.

Extra Special Spaghetti

4–5 boneless, skinless chicken breast halves
1 tablespoon (15 ml) olive oil
2 green capsicums, seeded, julienned
1 onion, chopped
1 455-g (16-ounce) jar tomato pasta sauce
230 g (8 ounces) shredded mozzarella cheese
340 g (12 ounces) vermicelli (thin spaghetti) pasta, cooked, drained

- Cut each chicken breast in 2.5-cm (1-inch) strips and sprinkle with salt and pepper. Place in large sprayed frypan and cook on medium-high heat for about 7 minutes on each side. Transfer chicken to plate and keep warm.

- In same frypan with oil, cook capsicums and onion until tender for about 5 to 8 minutes. Add pasta sauce and chicken strips and bring to a boil. Reduce heat to medium-low and cook for 15 minutes. Add half mozzarella cheese and cook just until cheese melts.

- Place cooked pasta on serving platter and spoon chicken-sauce mixture over pasta. Sprinkle remaining cheese over top and serve immediately. Serves 8 to 10.

Arabs spread what we know today as dried pasta (prepared by boiling) around the Mediterranean in the 11th century. Until then, fresh pasta was the norm. Makkaroni *is the Arabic word for pasta.*

Family-Secret Chicken and Pasta

This is a great recipe to prepare ahead of time and freeze.

¼ cup (60 g) butter
½ cup (60 g) flour
½ teaspoon basil
½ teaspoon parsley
2 cups (500 ml) milk
1 115-g (4-ounce) can sliced
  mushrooms, drained
1 280-g (10-ounce) can cream
  of mushroom soup
1 roasted red capsicum, diced
2 pounds boneless, skinless
  chicken breast halves,
  cooked, diced
½ litre (14 ounces) chicken
  stock
455 g (16 ounces) fettuccini (medium
  egg noodles) pasta
1 cup (115 g) shredded cheddar
  cheese

- Preheat oven to 175° C (350° F).

- Melt butter in saucepan, add flour, herbs and ½ teaspoon salt and cook over medium heat. Add milk slowly and stir constantly until thick.

- Add mushrooms, mushroom soup, roasted red capsicum, chicken and chicken stock.

- Cook pasta in saucepan according to package directions. Drain.

- Mix pasta with sauce and stir gently. Pour mixture into 25 x 38-cm (10 x 15-inch) baking dish. Sprinkle with cheese and cover and refrigerate until baking time. Bake for 20 to 30 minutes until it heats thoroughly. Serves 8 to 10.

Farmhouse Dinner

230 g (8 ounces) fettuccini (medium
   egg noodles) pasta
4–5 boneless, skinless
   chicken breast halves
½ litre (14 ounces) chicken
   stock
2 cups (200 g) sliced celery
2 onions, chopped
1 green and 1 red capsicum,
   seeded, chopped
1 280-g (10-ounce) can cream
   of chicken soup
1 280-g (10-ounce) can cream
   of mushroom soup
1 cup (115 g) shredded cheese

- Cook pasta in saucepan in boiling water until barely tender and drain well. Cut chicken into thin slices.

- Combine pasta, chicken and stock in large, sprayed slow cooker and mix. (Make sure noodles separate and coat with stock.)

- Combine remaining ingredients in saucepan and heat just enough to mix well and add to slow cooker. Cover and cook on low for 4 to 6 hours. Serves 6.

There is a pasta museum in Pontedassio, Italy, which includes exhibits of antique pasta-making machines and other tools as well as many examples of pasta.

Great Crazy Lasagna

Chicken never got mixed up with any better ingredients!

1 tablespoon (15 ml) butter
½ onion, chopped
1 cup (70 g) fresh mushrooms,
    sliced
1 280-g (10-ounce) can cream
    of chicken soup
1 455-g (16-ounce) jar alfredo
    sauce
1 roasted red capsicum, diced
⅓ cup (75 ml) dry white wine
½ teaspoon dried basil
280 g (10 ounces) frozen chopped
    spinach, thawed
425 g (15 ounces) ricotta cheese
⅓ cup (35 g) grated parmesan
    cheese
1 egg, beaten
9 lasagna sheets, cooked
3–4 cups (420–560 g) cooked
    chicken, shredded
455 g (16 ounces) shredded cheddar
    cheese

- Preheat oven to 175° C (350° F).

- Melt butter and sauté onion and mushrooms in large frypan. Stir in soup, alfredo sauce, roasted red capsicum, wine and basil. Reserve one-third sauce for top of lasagna.

- Squeeze spinach between paper towels to completely remove excess moisture.

- Combine spinach, ricotta, parmesan and egg in bowl and mix well.

- Place 3 lasagna sheets in sprayed 25 x 38-cm (10 x 15-inch) baking dish. Make sure dish is full size with a depth of 6.5 cm (2½ inches).

- Layer each with half of remaining sauce, spinach-ricotta mixture and chicken. (The spinach-ricotta mixture will be fairly dry and you will have to pour it over sauce and spread out.)

continued next page...

continued...

- Sprinkle with 1½ cups (360 ml) cheddar cheese. Repeat layering.

- Top with last 3 lasagna sheets and reserved sauce.

- Cover and bake for 45 minutes.

- Uncover and sprinkle remaining cheese on top.

- Bake for additional 5 minutes or just until cheese melts. Let lasagna stand for 10 minutes before serving. Serves 10 to 12.

Favourite Budget Chicken

280-g (10-ounce) can cream
    of chicken soup
3 spring onions, chopped
2 sticks celery, sliced
3 cups (710 ml) white rice, cooked
1 roasted red capsicum, chopped
340 g (12 ounces) chicken packet
    deli meat
1 145-g (5-ounce) can evaporated
    milk
1½ cups (85 g) chow mein noodles

- Preheat oven to 175° C (350° F).

- Combine soup, onions, celery, rice, roasted red capsicum, chicken, ½ cup water and evaporated milk in large bowl; mix until they blend well.

- Spoon into sprayed 2-L (2-quart) baking dish, cover and bake for 30 minutes. Serve over noodles. Serves 4 to 5.

Garden Chicken

This colourful, delicious casserole is not only flavour packed, but it is also a sight to behold! You can't beat this bountiful dish for family or company.

4 boneless, skinless chicken
    breast halves, cut
    into strips
1 teaspoon minced garlic
5 tablespoons (75 g) butter
1 small yellow squash,
    thinly sliced
1 small zucchini, thinly sliced
1 red capsicum, seeded,
    thinly sliced
4 tablespoons (30 g) flour
2 teaspoons pesto
½-litre (14-ounce) carton chicken
    stock
1 cup (310 g) unthickened cream
230 g (8 ounces) capelli
    d'angelo (angel hair)
    pasta, cooked al dente,
    drained
⅓ cup (335 g) shredded parmesan
    cheese

- Preheat oven to 175° C (350° F).

- Sauté chicken and garlic with 2 tablespoons (30 g) butter in large frypan over medium heat for about 15 minutes. Remove chicken and set aside.

- With butter in frypan, sauté squash, zucchini and capsicum and cook just until tender but crisp.

- Melt 3 tablespoons (45 ml) butter and add flour, pesto and ½ teaspoon each of salt and pepper in small saucepan. Stir to form smooth paste.

- Gradually add stock, stirring constantly over medium-high heat until thick. Stir in cream and heat thoroughly.

- Combine chicken, vegetables, stock-cream mixture and drained pasta in large bowl. Transfer to sprayed 23 x 33-cm (9 x 13-inch) baking dish.

- Cover and bake for 30 minutes.

- Uncover and sprinkle parmesan cheese over top of casserole and return to oven for additional 5 minutes. Serves 8.

Harmony with Linguine

340 g (12 ounces) linguine (thin egg
    noodles) pasta
2 teaspoons minced garlic
2 tablespoons (30 ml) olive oil
455 g (16 ounces) frozen broccoli
    florets, cauliflower and carrots
280 g (10 ounces) frozen baby green
    peas
455 g (1 pound) chicken pieces
2 tablespoons (30 g) butter
3 tablespoons (45 ml) light soy
    sauce
½ cup (10 g) fresh chopped
    coriander

- Cook pasta in saucepan according to package directions. Drain and stir in garlic and oil. Allow to cool for about 10 minutes.

- Bring large pot of water to a boil. Immerse all vegetables in water for about 30 seconds. Drain and set aside.

- Cut chicken in strips and cook chicken with butter and soy sauce in frypan for about 10 to 15 minutes or until juices run clear.

- Combine pasta, vegetables and chicken pieces in large bowl and toss to mix well. Transfer to serving dish and garnish with fresh coriander. Serves 8.

While there are many ancient indications of pasta-making from China, Greece, Rome and the Middle East, the Italians are the acknowledged masters of pasta-making today.

Hearty Chicken-Macaroni Casserole

1 onion, chopped
1 red capsicum, chopped
¼ cup (60 g) butter
1 280-g (10-ounce) can cream
    of chicken soup
1 roasted red capsicum, chopped
230 g (8 ounces) elbow
    macaroni (tube) pasta,
    cooked
3 cups (420 g) cooked, diced
    chicken
425 g (15 ounces) ricotta cheese
230 g (8 ounces) shredded cheddar
    cheese
¾ cup (45 g) crushed round,
    dry biscuits

- Preheat oven to 175° C (350° F).

- Sauté onions and capsicum with butter in frypan. Stir in soup and roasted red capsicum and mix.

- Combine pasta, chicken and cheeses in large bowl; mix until they blend well. Fold in soup-roasted red capsicum mixture and mix well.

- Spoon into sprayed 23 x 33-cm (9 x 13-inch) baking dish and bake for 40 minutes. Remove from oven and sprinkle crushed biscuits over top of casserole and cook for additional 15 minutes. Serves 10.

Lemony Chicken and Pappardelle

230 g (8 ounces) pappardelle (wide
    egg noodles) pasta
280 g (10 ounces) frozen
    snowpeas, thawed
½ litre (14 ounces) chicken
    stock
1 teaspoon fresh grated
    lemon peel
2 cups (280 g) cubed, skinless
    rotisserie chicken meat
½ cup (40 g) pouring cream

- Cook pasta in saucepan according to package directions. Add snowpeas to pasta 1 minute before pasta is done. Drain and return to saucepan.

- Add chicken stock, lemon peel, chicken pieces and ½ teaspoon each of salt and pepper. Heat, stirring constantly, until thoroughly hot.

- Over low heat, gently stir in cream. Serve hot. Serves 6.

Mac Cheese and Chicken

1½ cups (155 g) elbow macaroni
    (tube) pasta
1 340-g (12-ounce) can evaporated
    milk
½–⅔ cup (120–175 g) hot
    salsa
2 cups (280 g) skinned, cut-up
    roast chicken
230 g (8 ounces) cubed
    processed cheese

- Cook pasta in 2 cups (500 ml) water in saucepan according to package directions and drain well. Add evaporated milk and salsa and cook over medium heat for about 10 minutes, stirring frequently. (There will still be liquid in mixture.)

- Stir in roast chicken and heat until chicken heats thoroughly. Fold in cheese, stir constantly and cook for 1 minute. Serve immediately. Serves 8.

Mr. Mozz's Spaghetti

This is a wonderful casserole to serve to family or for company. It has great flavour and taste with chicken, pasta and colourful vegetables all in one dish. It's a winner, I promise!

1 bunch fresh spring onions
   with tops, chopped
1 cup (100 g) celery, chopped
1 red capsicum, seeded,
   chopped
1 yellow or orange capsicum, seeded,
   chopped
¼ cup (60 g) butter
1 tablespoon (15 ml) dried
   coriander leaves
1 teaspoon Italian seasoning
200 g (7 ounces) vermicelli (thin
   spaghetti) pasta,
   cooked, drained
4 cups (560 g) cooked chicken or
   turkey, chopped
230 g (8 ounces) sour
   cream
1 455-g (16-ounce) jar creamy
   pasta sauce

280 g (10 ounces) frozen green peas,
   thawed
230 g (8 ounces) shredded
   mozzarella cheese

- Preheat oven to 175° C (350° F).

- Sauté onions, celery and capsicums in large frypan with butter.

- Combine onion-capsicum mixture, coriander, Italian seasoning, a little salt and pepper, pasta, chicken, sour cream and pasta sauce in large bowl and mix well.

- Fold in peas and half mozzarella cheese.

- Spoon into sprayed 25 cm x 38-cm (10 x 15-inch) deep baking dish. Cover and bake for 45 minutes.

- Uncover and sprinkle remaining cheese over casserole. Return to oven for about 5 minutes. Serves 10 to 12.

TIP: With spaghetti dishes like this, break up the spaghetti before cooking it. That way it makes it a little easier to serve and to eat.

Mushrooms, Pasta and Chicken Casserole

½ cup (115 g) butter
1 green capsicum,
    seeded, chopped
1 red capsicum, seeded,
    chopped
½ cup (60 g) flour
1½ teaspoons seasoned salt
1½ cups (375 ml) milk
½ litre (14 ounces) beef
    stock
1 280-g (10-ounce) can cream
    of mushroom soup
340 g (12 ounces) fettuccini (medium
    egg noodles) pasta,
    cooked, drained
3–4 cups (420–560 g) cooked, cubed
    chicken
230 g (8 ounces) shredded cheddar
    cheese

• Preheat oven to 175° C (350° F).

• Melt butter in large frypan on medium-high heat. Cook and stir capsicums for 10 minutes. Stir in flour and seasoned salt and mix well.

• While still on medium-high heat, slowly stir in milk, beef stock and 1 teaspoon pepper. Cook until mixture is thick and pour into large bowl.

• Fold in mushroom soup, pasta and chicken and transfer to sprayed 25 x 38-cm (10 x 15-inch) baking dish.

• Cover and bake for 35 minutes or until thoroughly hot. Uncover, sprinkle cheese over casserole and return to oven for additional 5 minutes. Serves 12.

Mushroom-
Spaghetti Bake

230 g (8 ounces) spaghetti pasta
¼ cup (60 ml) olive oil
2 teaspoons minced garlic
230 g (8 ounces) fresh
   mushrooms, sliced
2½ cups (350 g) bite-size chunks
   roast chicken
¼ cup (30 g) capers, drained
1 cup (150 g) roasted red
   capsicum, drained
1 cup (115 g) shredded mozzarella
   cheese

- Cook pasta in saucepan according to package directions. Use ladle to remove carefully ½ cup (125 ml) hot water from saucepan and set aside. Drain pasta and rinse in hot water; set aside.

- Heat oil in large frypan over medium heat and cook garlic for about 2 minutes. Add mushrooms and cook for an additional 4 minutes. Raise heat to high and add chicken, capers and a little salt and pepper; cook for about 2 minutes, stirring often.

- Add reserved pasta liquid, pasta and stir to blend well. Cook for about 3 minutes or until mixture is thoroughly hot. Remove from heat and stir in roasted red capsicum and cheese. Serve immediately. Serves 4 to 6.

Noodle Chicken

85 g (3 ounces) chicken-flavoured, instant ramen noodles
455 g (16 ounces) frozen broccoli florets, cauliflower and carrots
⅔ cup (150 ml) sweet-and-sour sauce
3 boneless, skinless chicken breast halves, cooked

- Cook noodles and vegetables in saucepan with 2 cups (500 ml) boiling water for 3 minutes, stir occasionally and drain.

- Combine noodle-vegetable mixture with seasoning packet, sweet-and-sour sauce and a little salt and pepper. Cut chicken in strips, add chicken to noodle mixture and heat thoroughly. Serves 6.

TIP: You may want to add 1 tablespoon (15 ml) soy sauce, if you have it on hand.

Spaghetti Toss

280 g (10 ounces) spaghetti pasta
½ cup (70 g) frozen green peas, thawed
2 tablespoons (30 g) butter
3 cups (420 g) roast chicken
1 310-g (11-ounce) can mandarin oranges, drained
⅔ cup (150 ml) stir-fry sauce
2 teaspoons minced garlic

- Cook pasta in saucepan according to package directions. Stir in peas and cook for an additional 1 minute.

- Drain and stir in butter and garlic until butter is melted. Spoon into bowl. Cut chicken into strips and add strips, oranges and stir-fry sauce. Toss to coat. Serves 6 to 8.

Old-Fashioned Chicken Spaghetti

*This is also a great recipe
for leftover turkey.*

230 g (8–10 ounces) spaghetti pasta
1 capsicum, seeded, chopped
1 onion, chopped
1 cup (100 g) chopped celery
½ cup (120 g) butter
1 280-g (10-ounce) can
    tomato soup
1 280-g (10-ounce) can
    diced tomatoes
2 chopped green chillies
1 115-g (4-ounce) can chopped
    mushrooms
½ teaspoon garlic powder
3 chicken stock cubes
4–5 cups (560–700 g) chopped
    chicken or turkey
230 g (8 ounces) cubed mozzarella
    cheese
230 g (8 ounces) shredded cheddar
    cheese

- Preheat oven to 160° C (325° F).

- Cook pasta in saucepan according to package directions and drain.

- Sauté capsicum, onion and celery in butter in medium saucepan.

- Add soup, tomatoes, green chillies, mushrooms, garlic powder, stock cubes and ½ cup (125 ml) water and mix well.

- Mix pasta, soup, tomato mixture, chicken and cheese in large mixing bowl. Place in sprayed 2 (2-L/2-quart) baking dishes.

- Cover and bake for 40 to 50 minutes. Serves 10 to 12.

TIP: *Freeze one dish for later. To bake frozen dish, thaw first.*

Pecan-Topped Fettuccini

455 g (1 pound) boneless, skinless chicken breast halves
¾ cup (170 g) butter
230 g (8 ounces) mushrooms, sliced
1 bunch fresh spring onions, sliced
1 teaspoon minced garlic
230 g (8 ounces) wholemeal fettuccini (medium egg noodles) pasta
1 egg yolk
⅔ cup (210 g) unthickened cream
1 teaspoon (5 ml) dried parsley
½ cup (50 g) grated parmesan cheese
¾ cup (85 g) chopped pecans, toasted

- Cut chicken into 2.5-cm (1-inch) strips. Melt ¼ cup (55 g) butter in large frypan and cook chicken until light brown. Remove chicken from frypan and set aside.

- Leave pan drippings in frypan and cook mushrooms, onions, garlic and a little salt and pepper until vegetables are tender. Return chicken to frypan, mix well and simmer on low heat for 20 to 25 minutes or until chicken is done.

- Cook pasta in saucepan according to package directions and drain.

- Melt remaining butter and let cook before combining with egg yolk, cream and parsley. Stir this mixture into cooked pasta.

- Add cheese and toss until they blend well. Stir in chicken-vegetable mixture and toss. Spoon onto hot serving platter and sprinkle with toasted pecans. Serves 6.

Pa's Pleasing Pasta

400 g (14 ounces) frozen, crumbed chicken cutlets, thawed

1 795-g (28-ounce) jar spaghetti sauce

290 g (10 ounces) grated parmesan cheese

230 g (8 ounces) vermicelli (thin spaghetti) pasta, cooked

- Preheat oven to 205° C (400° F).

- Place cutlets in sprayed 23 x 33-cm (9 x 13-inch) baking dish and top each with about ¼ cup (60 ml) spaghetti sauce and a heaped tablespoon (15 ml) parmesan. Bake for 15 minutes.

- Place cooked pasta on serving platter and top with cutlets. Sprinkle remaining cheese over cutlets. Heat remaining spaghetti sauce and serve with chicken and spaghetti. Serves 8.

Quick Meal Fix

200 g (7 ounces) instant macaroni and cheese

¼ cup (60 g) butter

½ cup (125 ml) milk

280 g (10 ounces) frozen broccoli florets, thawed

2 cups (280 g) bite-size chunks roast chicken

1 cup (115 g) shredded sharp cheddar cheese

1 roasted red capsicum, chopped

- Prepare macaroni and cheese in saucepan according to package directions, but increase butter to ¼ cup (60 g) and milk to ½ cup (125 ml). Add at end of cooking time.

- Add cheese sauce mix and broccoli; stir to blend well. Stir in chicken, cheese and roasted red capsicum; mix well.

- Place mixture in microwave-safe bowl and heat on full power, for about 2 minutes. Stir well for flavours to blend well. Serves 4 to 6.

Rich Chicken Florentine

1 teaspoon minced garlic
4 boneless, skinless chicken
  breast halves,
  cut in strips
3 tablespoons (45 ml) olive oil
455 g (16 ounces) frozen spinach,
  thawed
130 g (4.5 ounces) alfredo sauce
2 tablespoons (30 ml) pesto
230 g (8 ounces) capelli
  d'angelo (angel hair) pasta
¼ cup (30 g) shredded mozzarella
  cheese

- Cook garlic and chicken strips with oil in large frypan over medium-high heat for about 8 minutes on each side. When chicken is no longer pink, add spinach and sauté all together for about 4 minutes.

- Pour alfredo sauce in saucepan, stir in pesto, warm through and set aside.

- Cook pasta in large saucepan until al dente. Rinse in cold water and drain. Add chicken-spinach mixture to pasta and toss with pesto-alfredo sauce. Mix well and top with mozzarella cheese. Serves 8.

Capelli d'angelo literally means 'angel hair' in Italian.

Robust Cajun Chicken

230 g (8 ounces) linguine
   (thin egg noodles) pasta
4 small boneless, skinless
   chicken breast halves
1 heaped tablespoon (15 ml) Cajun
   seasoning
3 tablespoons (40 g) butter
1 red capsicum, seeded, sliced
1 green capsicum, seeded,
   sliced
230 g (8 ounces) fresh mushrooms,
   stems removed
1½ cups (115 g) pouring cream
1 teaspoon dried basil
1 teaspoon lemon pepper
2 teaspoons minced garlic
½ cup (50 g) grated parmesan
   cheese

- Cook pasta until al dente according to package directions, drain and set aside. Keep warm.

- Place chicken on cutting board, cut each breast into about 4 strips and place in resealable plastic bag. Add Cajun seasoning and shake to coat.

- Melt butter in large frypan on medium-high heat and cook chicken until tender, about 8 minutes. Add capsicums and mushrooms, cook and stir for an additional 3 minutes.

- Reduce heat to medium and stir in cream, basil, lemon pepper and garlic. Cook until mixture is thoroughly hot. Add cooked pasta, toss while mixture is still on medium heat. Heat just until mixture is thoroughly hot.

- Serve right from frypan or transfer to serving bowl and sprinkle with parmesan cheese. Serves 8.

Rotini Chicken

1 litre (28 ounces) chicken
  stock
1 teaspoon minced garlic
340 g (12 ounces) rotini (spiral)
  pasta
455 g (16 ounces) frozen broccoli
  florets, cauliflower, carrots
455 g (1 pound) chicken pieces,
  halved
1–2 teaspoons Italian
  seasoning
2 tablespoons (30 ml) olive oil
⅓ cup (40 g) shredded
  mozzarella cheese

- Combine stock, garlic and ½ cup (125 ml) water in large saucepan and bring to a boil. Add pasta, reduce heat to medium-low and cook for about 10 minutes or until tender.

- Add vegetables and bring to a boil again. Reduce heat to medium and cook for 10 minutes or until vegetables are tender.

- Sprinkle chicken pieces with Italian seasoning and ½ teaspoon pepper. Cook chicken in frypan with oil for about 10 minutes and turn once.

- Add chicken to pasta-vegetable mixture and heat on low until thoroughly hot. Spoon mixture onto serving platter and sprinkle cheese over top. Serve immediately. Serves 8 to 10.

Savoury Chicken Fettuccini

910 g (2 pounds) boneless, skinless chicken thighs, cubed
½ teaspoon garlic powder
1 red capsicum, seeded, chopped
2 sticks celery, chopped
1 280-g (10-ounce) can cream of celery soup
1 280-g (10-ounce) can cream of chicken soup
230 g (8 ounces) cubed cheddar cheese
1 roasted red capsicum, diced
455 g (16 ounces) spinach fettuccini (medium egg noodles) pasta

- Place chicken in sprayed slow cooker. Sprinkle with garlic powder, ½ teaspoon pepper, capsicum and celery. Mix soups (no water) in bowl and pour on chicken.

- Cover and cook on high for 4 to 6 hours or until chicken juices are clear. Stir in cheese and roasted red capsicum. Cover and cook until cheese melts.

- Cook pasta in saucepan according to package directions and drain. Place pasta in serving bowl and spoon chicken over pasta. Serve hot. Serves 10.

Spicy Orange Chicken over Noodles

455 g (1 pound) boneless, skinless chicken pieces
2 tablespoons (30 ml) olive oil
2 tablespoons (30 ml) soy sauce
455 g (16 ounces) frozen stir-fry vegetables, thawed
⅔ cup (210 g) orange marmalade
1 tablespoon (15 ml) olive oil
1 tablespoon (15 ml) soy sauce
1½ teaspoons lime juice
½ teaspoon minced ginger
½ teaspoon cayenne pepper
170 g (6 ounces) chow mein noodles, cooked

- Lightly brown chicken pieces in oil in large frypan over medium-high heat. Add soy sauce and cook for additional 3 minutes.

- Add stir-fry vegetables and cook for about 5 minutes or until vegetables are tender but crisp.

- Combine marmalade, oil, soy sauce, lime juice, ginger and cayenne pepper in saucepan and mix well.

- Heat and pour over stir-fry chicken and vegetables. Serve over chow mein noodles. Serves 8.

Warming plates before serving pasta helps the food remain warm while being eaten. Put plates or dishes in a 120° C (250° F) oven for 10 or 15 minutes. Or pour hot water into dishes and let stand until ready to use; then dry the bowls and serve the pasta.

Stir-Fry Cashew Chicken

Olive oil
455 g (1 pound) chicken strips
455 g (16 ounces) frozen broccoli
    florets, cauliflower and carrots
1 230-g (8-ounce) jar stir-fry sauce
⅓ cup (45 g) cashew halves
340 g (12 ounces) chow
    mein noodles, cooked

- Place a little oil and stir-fry chicken strips in 32-cm (12-inch) wok or frypan over high heat for about 4 minutes.

- Add vegetables and stir-fry for additional 4 minutes or until vegetables are tender. Stir in stir-fry sauce and cashews and cook just until mixture is hot. Serve over noodles. Serves 6.

Stir-Fry Chicken

Olive oil
455 g (1 pound) chicken strips
455 g (16 ounces) frozen broccoli
    florets, cauliflower and carrots
1 230-g (8-ounce) jar stir-fry sauce
340 g (12 ounces) chow
    mein noodles, cooked
1 red capsicum
1 teaspoon chopped fresh coriander

- Place a little oil and stir-fry chicken strips in 32-cm (12-inch) wok over high heat for about 4 minutes.

- Add vegetables and stir-fry for additional 4 minutes or until vegetables are tender. Stir in stir-fry sauce and cook just until mixture is hot. Serve over noodles and sprinkle with coriander. Serves 6.

Stir-Fry Chicken Spaghetti

455 g (1 pound) boneless, skinless
  chicken breast halves
Olive oil
1½ cups (105 g) sliced mushrooms
1½ cups (135 g) capsicum strips
1 cup (250 ml) sweet-and-sour
  stir-fry sauce
455 g (16 ounces) spaghetti pasta,
  cooked
¼ cup (60 g) butter

• Season chicken with salt and
  pepper and cut into thin slices.
  Brown chicken slices in large
  frypan with a little oil on medium-
  low heat and cook for 5 minutes.
  Transfer to plate and set aside.

• In same frypan with a little more
  oil, stir-fry mushrooms and
  capsicum strips for 5 minutes. Add
  chicken strips and sweet-and-sour
  sauce and stir until ingredients
  are hot.

• Prepare pasta according to package
  directions. While pasta is still hot,
  drain well, add butter and stir until
  butter melts. Place in large bowl
  and toss with chicken mixture.
  Serve hot. Serves 8.

Sweet-and-Sour Chicken-Veggies

10 g (3 ounces) chicken-flavoured
  ramen noodles
455 g (16 ounces) frozen broccoli
  florets, cauliflower and carrots
⅔ cup (150 ml) sweet-and-sour sauce
1 tablespoon (15 ml) soy sauce
3 boneless, skinless, cooked
  chicken breast halves,
  cut in strips (can use
  deli turkey)

• Cook noodles and vegetables in
  2 cups (500 ml) water (set aside
  seasoning packet) in large
  saucepan for 3 minutes or until
  liquid is absorbed.

• Add seasoning packet, chicken
  (or turkey), sweet-and-sour sauce,
  soy sauce and a little salt and
  pepper. Heat on medium-low heat,
  stirring until all is thoroughly hot.
  Serves 6.

Tantalising Chicken Alfredo

340 g (12 ounces) fettuccini (medium
    egg noodles) pasta
4 tablespoons (60 ml) extra-virgin
    olive oil
⅔ cup (110 g) finely chopped spring
    onions
½ cup (75 g) finely chopped
    capsicum
4–5 large boneless, skinless
    chicken breast halves
1 tablespoon (15 ml) minced garlic
1 litre (1 quart) pouring cream
¼ cup (60 g) butter
1 tablespoon (15 ml) Italian
    seasoning
½ cup (50 g) grated romano cheese

- Cook pasta in saucepan according
  to package directions. Rinse, drain
  and place in large bowl. Drizzle
  2 tablespoons (30 ml) olive oil over
  pasta and stir to coat every strand.
  Set aside.

- Heat remaining oil in large frypan
  or soup pot and quickly sauté
  onions and capsicum just until they
  are slightly softened. Remove from
  pot and set aside.

- Cut chicken into thin slices and
  place chicken and garlic in pot and
  sauté for about 5 minutes. (Add
  more oil if needed.) Spoon onion-
  capsicum mixture back into pot and
  stir until mixture blends well.

- Turn heat to high, pour in cream
  and cook, stirring constantly,
  until mixture thickens. Add
  butter and Italian seasoning and
  continue stirring until mixture is
  semi-thick paste.

- Reduce heat to medium-low and
  simmer for 10 minutes. Fold pasta
  into chicken-cream mixture and
  heat on medium just until mixture
  is thoroughly hot. Sprinkle with
  cheese and serve immediately.
  Serves 8 to 10.

Thank Goodness Chicken

4 boneless, skinless chicken
   breast halves
2 tablespoons (30 g) butter
2 tablespoons (15 g) flour
2 tablespoons (30 ml) French onion
   soup mix
1¼ cups (390 g) unthickened cream
455 g (16 ounces) fettuccini (medium
   egg noodles) pasta
¼ cup (15 g) finely shredded
   parmesan cheese

- Cut chicken into bite-size pieces. Melt butter in frypan and cook chicken until juices run clear and outside browns evenly.

- Sprinkle flour and soup mix over chicken and stir well. Stir in cream and cook, stirring constantly, until it thickens and bubbles.

- Cook pasta in saucepan according to package directions. Drain and place on serving platter. Spoon creamy chicken mixture over pasta; sprinkle with cheese and serve immediately. Serves 8.

Rule-the-Roost Casserole

200 g (7 ounces) instant pasta and
   sauce with chicken flavour
1 280-g (10-ounce) can cream
   of mushroom soup
1 280-g (10-ounce) can cream
   of celery soup
3 cups (420 g) cooked, chopped
   chicken or turkey
280 g (10 ounces) frozen peas,
   thawed
1 cup (115 g) shredded cheddar
   cheese

- Preheat oven to 175° C (350° F).

- Cook pasta and sauce in saucepan according to package directions.

- Mix both soups with ½ cup (125 ml) water in bowl.

- Combine chicken, cooked pasta and sauce, soups, peas and cheese and mix well.

- Pour into sprayed 3-L (3-quart) baking dish. Cover and bake for 40 minutes. Serves 8.

Three-Cheese Chicken Pasta

1 cup (60 g) fine breadcrumbs
6 boneless, skinless chicken
    breast halves
2 eggs, beaten
¼ cup (60 g) butter
1 425-g (15-ounce) bottle
    tomato pasta sauce
½ cup (125 ml) evaporated milk
3 slices mozzarella cheese,
    halved crosswise
6 slices Swiss cheese
2 tablespoons (15 g) grated
    parmesan cheese
340 g (12 ounces) fettuccini (medium
    egg noodles) pasta

- Preheat oven to 175° C (350° F).

- Combine breadcrumbs and
  ½ teaspoon salt in shallow bowl
  and set aside.

- In separate shallow bowl, place
  beaten eggs and dip each chicken
  breast in eggs and breadcrumbs.
  Melt butter in large frypan over
  medium heat.

- Add chicken breasts, one at a time,
  and cook for about 2 minutes on
  each side or until golden brown.
  Remove chicken and drain.

- Combine pasta sauce and
  evaporated milk in small bowl and
  mix well. Reserve ¼ cup (60 ml)
  plus 2 tablespoons (30 ml) and
  set aside. Pour remaining sauce
  mixture into sprayed 23 x 33-cm
  (9 x 13-inch) baking pan. Place
  each chicken breast in baking pan,
  cover and bake for 25 minutes.

- Remove from oven and place slices
  of mozzarella and Swiss cheese on
  each chicken breast half. Top with
  1 tablespoon (15 ml) reserved sauce
  and sprinkle with parmesan cheese.
  Cover and bake for an additional
  5 minutes.

- Cook pasta in saucepan according
  to package directions, drain and
  place on hot serving platter. Top
  with chicken breasts and remaining
  sauce. Serves 6.

Tortellini-Chicken Dinner

255 g (9 ounces) refrigerated
　cheese-filled tortellini pasta
280 g (10 ounces) frozen green peas,
　thawed
230 g (8 ounces) cream
　cheese with chives and onion
½ cup (120 g) sour cream
255 g (9 ounces) frozen,
　cooked chicken breast strips

- Cook pasta in saucepan according
to package directions. Place peas in
colander and pour hot pasta water
over peas. Return pasta and peas to
saucepan.

- In separate small saucepan,
combine cream cheese and sour
cream, heat on low and stir well
until cream cheese melts. Spoon
mixture over pasta and peas, toss
and keep heat on low.

- Heat cooked chicken in microwave
according to package directions.
Spoon pasta and peas in serving
bowl and place chicken on top.
Serve hot. Serves 6.

Vermicelli Toss

280 g (10 ounces) vermicelli (thin
　spaghetti) pasta
280 g (10 ounces) frozen snowpeas
2 tablespoons (30 g) butter
3 cups (420 g) roast chicken strips
1 310-g (11-ounce) can mandarin
　oranges, drained
⅔ cup (150 ml) stir-fry sauce
½ cup (70 g) frozen corn kernels

- Cook pasta in saucepan according
to package directions. Stir in peas
and corn and cook for additional
1 minute. Drain and stir in butter
until butter melts. Spoon into bowl.

- Add chicken strips, oranges
and stir-fry sauce. Toss to coat.
Serves 6.

Winner's Circle Pasta

340 g (12 ounces) wholemeal
    rotini (spiral) pasta
4 boneless, skinless
    chicken breast halves
Lemon pepper
1 teaspoon minced garlic
2 tablespoons (30 ml) olive oil
1 cup (10 ounces) chicken stock
280 g (10 ounces) frozen green peas,
    thawed
225 g (32 ounces) shredded carrots
85 g (3 ounces) cream cheese
2 teaspoons lemon juice
½ cup (50 g) grated parmesan
    cheese

- Cook pasta in saucepan according to package directions, drain and keep warm.

- Cut chicken into strips, sprinkle liberally with lemon pepper and place in large frypan. Add garlic and oil; cook on medium-high heat until chicken juices are clear. Remove from frypan and keep warm.

- In same frypan, add stock, peas, carrots, cream cheese and lemon juice, cook and stir until cheese melts. Stir pasta and chicken into vegetable mixture and heat thoroughly. Sprinkle with parmesan cheese. Serve right from the frypan. Serves 4 to 6.

Spaghetti Tango

2 tablespoons (30 ml) olive oil
1 onion, chopped
1 red capsicum, chopped
2 teaspoons minced garlic
455 g (1 pound) turkey or chicken
    sausages
2 425-g (15-ounce) cans Italian
    stewed tomatoes
2 chopped green chillies
1 teaspoon dried basil
230 g (8 ounces) vermicelli (thin
    spaghetti) pasta,
    cooked, drained
½ cup (120 ml) grated parmesan
    cheese

- Heat oil in large frypan on medium-high heat and cook onions, capsicums and garlic for about 6 minutes. Remove casing on sausage and add to frypan. Break up sausage with fork and cook for 5 minutes.

- Stir in tomatoes, green chillies, basil, and a little salt and pepper. Bring to a boil, reduce heat to medium-low, stirring often, and simmer for 30 minutes. While sauce cooks, break up tomatoes with back of spoon.

- Place hot pasta on serving platter and spoon sausage-tomato mixture over pasta. Sprinkle parmesan cheese over top; serve immediately. Serves 6 to 8.

The availability of electricity in the early 20th century made the labour-intensive process of manufacturing pasta easier and more economical.

3-Cheese Turkey Casserole

230 g (8 ounces) fettuccini (medium
    egg noodles) pasta
1 teaspoon olive oil
3 tablespoons (90 g) butter
¾ cup (110 g) green capsicum,
    chopped
½ cup (50 g) celery, chopped
½ cup (80 g) onion, chopped
1 280-g (10-ounce) can cream
    of chicken soup
½ cup (125 ml) milk
1 170-g (6-ounce) jar whole
    mushrooms
455 g (16 ounces) cottage cheese
4 cups (560 g) diced turkey or
    chicken
340 g (12 ounces) shredded cheddar
    cheese
¾ cup (75 g) freshly grated
    parmesan cheese

- Preheat oven to 175° C (350° F).

- Combine pasta in 3 L (3 quarts)
  hot water, add 1 tablespoon
  (15 ml) salt and oil in large
  soup pot and cook according to
  package directions.

- Melt butter in frypan and sauté
  capsicum, celery and onion.

- Combine pasta, capsicum-onion
  mixture, chicken soup, milk,
  mushrooms, ½ teaspoon pepper,
  cottage cheese, turkey and cheddar
  cheese in large bowl.

- Pour into sprayed 23 x 33-cm
  (9 x 13-inch) baking dish and top
  with parmesan cheese. Bake for
  40 minutes. Serves 8.

Stuffed Turkey Shells

28 5-cm (2-inch) gigantoni (extra large tubes) pasta
455 g (1 pound) minced turkey
½ cup (80 g) finely minced onion
½ cup (30 g) breadcrumbs
½ cup (50 g) grated parmesan cheese
3 eggs, beaten
280 g (10 ounces) frozen chopped spinach, thawed, drained
1 425-g (15-ounce) jar tomato pasta sauce
230 g (8 ounces) shredded mozzarella cheese

- Preheat oven at 175° C (350° F).

- Cook pasta in saucepan according to package directions, drain and place on strip of baking paper where shells will not touch.

- Brown turkey and onion in large frypan; drain fat. Add breadcrumbs, parmesan cheese, eggs, spinach and a little salt and pepper; mix well. Carefully stuff mixture into shells and set aside.

- Spoon 1 cup (250 ml) sauce into sprayed 2 to 3-L (2 to 3-quart) baking dish. Arrange stuffed shells over sauce and pour remaining sauce over shells.

- Top with mozzarella, cover and bake for 40 minutes or until mixture is hot and bubbly. Uncover for last 5 minutes of cooking time. Serves 6 to 8.

Tempting Turkey over Fettuccini

1 tablespoon (15 ml) olive oil
2 teaspoons minced garlic
2 425-g (15-ounce) cans Italian
    stewed tomatoes
2 green chillies, chopped
½ teaspoon sugar
⅔ cup (50 g) pouring cream
455 g (1 pound) deli smoked
    turkey breast, cut into
    thin strips
2 tablespoons (10 g) chopped
    fresh parsley
230 g (8 ounces) wholemeal
    fettuccini (medium
    egg noodles) pasta
¼ cup (25 g) grated parmesan
    cheese

- Heat oil in large frypan and sauté garlic 1 minute. Add stewed tomatoes and green chillies and break tomatoes up by hand as you put them in frypan.

- Stir in sugar and a little salt and pepper. Bring mixture to a boil, reduce heat to medium and cook for 15 minutes, stirring often, until mixture thickens. Stir constantly over medium heat and gradually add cream, turkey and parsley. Remove from heat.

- Cook pasta in saucepan according to package directions, drain and place on serving platter. To serve, spoon tomato-turkey mixture over pasta and sprinkle with parmesan cheese. Serves 6.

Tri-Colour Pasta with Turkey Dinner

340 g (12 ounces) tri-colour fusilli
  (spiral) pasta
1 115-g (4-ounce) can sliced black
  olives, drained
1 cup (70 g) fresh broccoli florets
1 cup (100 g) cauliflower florets
2 small yellow squash, sliced
1 cup (150 g) halved cherry
  tomatoes
1 230-g (8-ounce) bottle ranch
  dressing
680 g (1½ pounds) sliced smoked
  cracked pepper turkey breast

- Cook pasta in saucepan according
  to package directions. Drain and
  rinse in cold water. Place in large
  salad bowl and add olives, broccoli,
  cauliflower, squash and tomatoes.
  Toss with dressing.

- Place thin slices of turkey breast,
  arranged in a row over salad. Serve
  immediately. Serves 6.

Turkey and Fettuccini

230 g (8 ounces) fettuccini (medium
  egg noodles) pasta
2½ cups (350 g) diced, cooked
  turkey
30 g (1 ounce) chicken gravy,
  prepared
2 cups (120 g) round, dry biscuit
  crumbs

- Preheat oven to 175° C (350° F).

- Boil pasta in saucepan according to
  package directions and drain.

- Arrange alternate layers of pasta,
  turkey and gravy in sprayed 2-L
  (2-quart) baking dish. Cover with
  biscuit crumbs.

- Bake for 35 minutes. Serves 6.

Turkey and Fettuccini Plus

340 g (12 ounces) fettuccini (medium
    egg noodles) pasta
3 cups (420 g) cooked, diced
    turkey
455 g (16 ounces) frozen peas and
    carrots, thawed
2 340-g (12-ounce) jars chicken
    simmer sauce
2 cups (110 g) slightly crushed
    potato chips

- Preheat oven to 175° C (350° F).

- Cook pasta in saucepan according
  to package directions and drain.

- Arrange alternate layers of pasta,
  turkey, peas and carrots, and sauce
  in sprayed 23 x 33-cm (9 x 13-inch)
  baking dish. Cover and bake for
  20 minutes.

- Remove from oven, sprinkle potato
  chips over casserole and return to
  oven for 15 minutes or until chips
  are light brown. Serves 12.

Turkey Spaghetti

910 g (2 pounds) minced turkey
2 280-g (10-ounce) cans tomato
    condensed soup
½ litre (14 ounces) chicken stock
400 g (14 ounces) spaghetti pasta,
    broken, cooked, drained
1 425-g (15-ounce) can whole corn
    kernels, drained
1 115-g (4-ounce) can sliced
    mushrooms, drained
¼ cup (70 g) tomato sauce

- Cook turkey and season with a little
  salt and pepper in non-stick frypan.
  Place cooked turkey in
  5 to 6-L (5 to 6-quart) slow cooker.
  Add in soups, stock, spaghetti,
  corn, mushrooms and tomato sauce
  and stir to blend.

- Cover and cook on low for
  5 to 7 hours or on high for
  3 hours. Serves 4 to 6.

Turkey Stuffed Capsicums

2 red capsicums
2 yellow capsicums
680 g (1½ pounds) minced turkey
½ onion, finely chopped
1 425-g (15-ounce) can Italian
    stewed tomatoes
½ cup (90 g) orzo (tiny) pasta
½ teaspoon dried oregano
½ teaspoon dried basil
½ teaspoon ground allspice
¾ cup (75 g) grated parmesan
    cheese

- Preheat oven to 190° C (375° F).

- Halve capsicums lengthwise and remove stem ends, seeds and membranes. Immerse in large pot of boiling water for 3 minutes.

- Remove capsicums with slotted spoon, sprinkle insides with a little salt and invert on paper towels to drain.

- Sauté turkey and onion in frypan over medium heat for about 5 minutes. Drain fat and stir in tomatoes, pasta, oregano, basil, allspice, a little salt and ½ cup (125 ml) water.

- Cover and cook on medium-low heat for 10 minutes.

- Stir in half parmesan cheese and mix until all ingredients mix well.

- Fill capsicum halves with turkey mixture and place in sprayed 3-L (3-quart) baking dish. Place any remaining meat mixture around capsicums. Bake for 15 minutes and sprinkle with remaining cheese. Serves 6 to 8.

Turkey Tetrazzini

¼ cup (60 g) butter
½ cup (80 g) onion, chopped
1 stick celery, chopped
¼ cup (30 g) flour
1 cup (250 ml) milk
1½ cups (10 ounces) chicken stock
½ teaspoon dried tarragon
1 teaspoon dried parsley
230 g (8 ounces) spaghetti pasta
2 cups (480 ml) cooked, chopped
   turkey
¾ cup (80 g) shredded Swiss
   cheese

- Preheat oven at 175° C (350° F).

- Melt butter in large frypan and sauté onion and celery for 2 minutes. On medium heat, add flour and stir well.

- Gradually add milk and chicken stock and stir constantly until mixture thickens and bubbles. Stir in tarragon, parsley and a little salt and pepper.

- Break pasta in half and cook in saucepan according to package directions and drain. Add pasta, turkey and ½ cup (55 g) cheese to onion-stock mixture and mix well.

- Spoon into sprayed 2-L (2-quart) baking dish, cover and bake for 25 minutes. Uncover and sprinkle remaining cheese over top and return to oven for 5 minutes. Serves 4 to 5.

Pasta
with Pork

From tenderloins to bacon, pork is perfect with pasta! Savoury recipes will make your family say 'yummy'!

Pasta with Pork

A Different Macaroni

230 g (8 ounces) macaroni (tube) pasta
½ cup (40 g) pouring cream
230 g (8 ounces) shredded gorgonzola cheese
280 g (10 ounces) frozen green peas, thawed
2 cups (280 g) cooked, cubed ham

- Cook pasta in saucepan according to package directions and drain. Add cream and gorgonzola cheese and stir until cheese melts.

- Fold in peas and ham and cook on low heat, stirring constantly, for 5 minutes or until mixture is thoroughly hot. Spoon into serving bowl and serve hot. Serves 10.

Absolute Alfredo Ham

255 g (9 ounces) refrigerated tortellini pasta
2 tablespoons (30 g) butter
1½ cups (210 g) cooked ham, cut in thin slices
280 g (10 ounces) frozen green peas, thawed
230 g (8 ounces) mushrooms, sliced
1 roasted red capsicum, chopped
1 455-g (16-ounce) jar alfredo pasta sauce

- Cook pasta in saucepan according to package directions; drain and set aside. Melt butter in large frypan over medium heat and stir in ham, peas, mushrooms, roasted red capsicum and a little salt and pepper.

- Add alfredo sauce and pasta and stir to mix well. Cover and let mixture simmer on low heat for about 5 to 6 minutes; serve immediately. Serves 4 to 6.

Bow-Tie
Ham Dinner

**230 g (8 ounces) farfalle
(bow-tie) pasta**
**230 g (8 ounces) chive and onion
cream cheese**
¾ cup (235 g) unthickened cream
**1 cup (135 g) baby carrots, cut in
half lengthwise**
**½ yellow capsicum,
seeded, julienned**
**1 230-g (8-ounce) can cut green
beans, drained**
2 cups (280 g) cooked ham strips
¼ teaspoon dried basil
**⅓ cup (35 g) grated parmesan
cheese**

- Cook pasta according to package directions and drain.

- Place cream cheese and cream in large sprayed frypan and cook over medium heat for 2 or 3 minutes, stirring constantly until mixture is smooth.

- Stir in carrots and capsicum and cook for about 5 minutes, stirring occasionally. Stir in green beans, ham and basil. Cook, stirring occasionally just until dish is thoroughly hot.

- Spoon into serving bowl and sprinkle top with parmesan cheese. Serves 8.

*Farfalle pasta is commonly called bow-tie because of its shape.
Farfalle actually means 'butterfly' in Italian. It's called* farfalle tonde
when the corners are rounded, and it's very attractive in salads.

Bow-Tie Pasta, Ham and Veggies

230 g (8 ounces) farfalle
    (bow-tie) pasta
280 g (10 ounces) each
    frozen broccoli florets
    and green peas, thawed
1 455-g (16-ounce) jar alfredo
    sauce
455 g (1 pound) cooked, cubed ham

- Cook pasta in large saucepan
  according to package directions.
  Add broccoli and peas during
  last 3 minutes of cooking time.
  Drain well.

- Add alfredo sauce and ham. (This
  is a good time to use that leftover
  ham.) Cook and stir gently over
  very low heat to keep ingredients
  from sticking to pan. Spoon into
  serving bowl. Serves 6.

TIP: To substitute with deli
      ham, have the butcher cut
      a thick slice and you cut
      ham into chunks.

Creamed Ham with Spaghetti

2 280-g (10-ounce) cans cream of
    mushroom soup
1 teaspoon minced garlic
1 cup (70 g) sliced fresh
    mushrooms
2–2½ cups (420–475 g) cooked,
    cubed ham
1 145-g (5-ounce) can
    evaporated milk
200 g (7 ounces) spaghetti pasta,
    broken

- Combine soups, garlic, mushrooms,
  ham, evaporated milk and a little
  salt and pepper in slow cooker.

- Cover and cook on low for
  2 hours and mix well after cooking.

- Cook pasta in saucepan and drain.
  Add pasta to slow cooker and toss
  to coat. Serves 4 to 6.

Ham and Pasta Bake

1 280-g (10-ounce) can cream of
    celery soup
½ cup (50 g) grated parmesan cheese
1 cup (250 ml) milk
1 tablespoon (15 ml) spicy brown
    mustard
455 g (16 ounces) frozen broccoli
    florets, thawed
2 cups (210 g) tube pasta, cooked
230 g (8 ounces) (deli) cooked ham,
    cut in bite-size chunks
Thin strips red capsicum for garnish

• Preheat oven to 175° C (350° F).

• Combine soup, milk and mustard
  in large frypan and mix well. Add
  broccoli and stir over medium heat.

• Reduce heat to low, cover and cook
  for 5 minutes or until broccoli is
  tender but crisp.

• Stir in pasta and ham and heat
  thoroughly. Transfer to sprayed
  2-L (2-quart) baking dish and
  sprinkle with parmesan cheese.
  Bake until cheese starts to brown.

• Garnish with very thin strips of
  capsicum. Serves 8 to 10.

Peppery Pasta and Peas

2 tablespoons (30 ml) olive oil
1 onion, chopped
1 425-g (15-ounce) can stewed
    tomatoes
1 teaspoon paprika
1 145-g (5-ounce) can evaporated
    milk
2 teaspoons dried basil
A scant ¼ teaspoon crushed
    red chilli flakes
230 g (8 ounces) farfalle (bow-tie)
    pasta, cooked, drained
1 230-g (8-ounce) can green peas,
    drained
1 cup (140 g) cooked, cubed ham
¼ cup (25 g) grated parmesan
    cheese

• Heat oil in large frypan and sauté
  onion for about 8 minutes. Add
  tomatoes, paprika, evaporated milk,
  basil, chilli and a little salt. Bring
  to a boil, reduce heat to low and
  simmer for about 10 minutes or
  until it thickens slightly. Stir often.

• Stir in cooked pasta, peas and ham
  and toss well. Place in serving bowl
  and sprinkle with parmesan cheese.
  Serves 4.

Ham, Linguine and the Works

230 g (8 ounces) linguine (thin egg noodles) pasta
2 280-g (10-ounce) cans cream of celery soup
230 g (8 ounces) pouring cream
1 230-g (8-ounce) can whole corn kernels, drained
455 g (16 ounces) frozen broccoli florets, cauliflower and carrots, thawed
3 cups (420 g) cooked, cubed ham
230 g (8 ounces) shredded cheddar cheese

- Preheat oven to 160° C (325° F).

- Cook pasta in saucepan according to package directions.

- Combine celery soup, cream, corn, broccoli-carrot mixture, ham and a little salt and pepper in large bowl. Fold in pasta and half of cheese.

- Spoon into sprayed 23 x 33-cm (9 x 13-inch) baking dish. Cover and bake for 45 minutes. Remove from oven, sprinkle remaining cheese over top and return to oven for 5 minutes. Serves 8.

When boiling pasta for a baked dish, reduce the cooking time because the pasta will finish cooking when the dish is baked. The pasta should be flexible but still firm; usually one-third to one-half the usual cooking time will be sufficient.

Ham-Linguine Special

2 teaspoons minced garlic
¾ cup (100 g) coarsely chopped
    walnuts
2 red capsicums, seeded, julienned
1 green capsicum, seeded, julienned
¼ cup (60 ml) olive oil
455 g (1 pound) cooked ham,
    cut in strips
1 455-g (16-ounce) jar creamy
    pasta sauce
1 230-g (8-ounce) carton sour
    cream
145 g (5 ounces) grated parmesan
    cheese
340 g (12 ounces) shredded
    mozzarella cheese
340 g (12 ounces) linguine (thin egg
    noodles) pasta, cooked
1½ cups (180 g) seasoned
    breadcrumbs
¼ cup (60 g) butter, melted

- Preheat oven to 160° C (325° F).

- Sauté garlic, walnuts and capsicums with oil in large frypan for 1 to 2 minutes.

- Combine garlic-capsicum mixture, ham, pasta sauce, sour cream, parmesan cheese and mozzarella cheese in large bowl; mix well.

- Gently fold in cooked pasta and spoon into sprayed 25 x 38-cm (10 x 15-inch) baking dish.

- Combine breadcrumbs and melted butter in bowl and sprinkle over top of casserole.

- Bake for 40 to 45 minutes or until breadcrumbs are light brown. Serves 20.

Linguine and Ham

230 g (8 ounces) wholemeal
    linguine (thin egg noodles)
    pasta
2 tablespoons (30 g) butter
½ cup (80 g) chopped onion
1–2 cups (140–280 g) cooked,
    chopped ham
½ litre (14 ounces) carton chicken
    stock
2 tablespoons (10 g) chopped
    fresh sage leaves
255 g (9 ounces) baby spinach
¼ cup (25 g) grated parmesan
    cheese

- Cook pasta in saucepan according to package directions, drain and keep warm.

- Melt butter in frypan and sauté onion for 5 minutes. Stir in ham, chicken stock and sage leaves; cook on medium-low heat for 2 minutes.

- Add spinach and cook just until spinach wilts. Add a little salt and pepper, toss ham-spinach mixture with pasta and serve with sprinkled parmesan cheese. Serves 8.

Mac 'n Cheese Casserole

4 eggs
1½ cups (375 ml) milk
340 g (12 ounces) macaroni (tube)
    pasta, cooked
230 g (8 ounces) shredded cheddar
    cheese
2 cups (280 g) cooked, cubed ham
¾ cup (90 g) seasoned
    breadcrumbs
¼ cup (60 g) butter, cubed

- Preheat oven to 175° C (350° F).

- Lightly beat eggs and milk with a little salt and pepper in large bowl. Stir in pasta, cheese and ham.

- Spoon into sprayed 18 x 28-cm (7 x 11-inch) baking dish and bake for 20 minutes. Remove from oven, sprinkle with breadcrumbs and dot with butter. Continue baking for additional 15 minutes. Serves 8.

Noodles-Ham Veggie Mix

230 g (8 ounces) fettuccini (medium egg noodles) pasta
2 280-g (10-ounce) cans cream of celery soup
1 280-g (10-ounce) can cream of broccoli soup
1 chicken stock cube
1½ cups (465 g) unthickened cream
1 230-g (8-ounce) can whole corn kernels, drained
455 g (16 ounces) frozen broccoli florets, cauliflower and carrots, thawed
3 cups (420 g) cooked cubed ham
230 g (8 ounces) shredded cheddar cheese

- Preheat oven to 175° C (350° F).

- Cook pasta in saucepan according to package directions and drain.

- Combine soups, chicken stock cube, cream, corn, broccoli-carrot mixture, ham, ½ teaspoon each of salt and pepper in large bowl and mix well.

- Fold in egg noodles and half of cheese.

- Spoon into sprayed 23 x 33-cm (9 x 13-inch) baking dish. Cover and bake for 45 minutes.

- Uncover and sprinkle remaining cheese over top of casserole. Return to oven and bake for additional 10 minutes or until cheese bubbles. Serves 8.

Picky Eater's Paradise Pie

230 g (8 ounces) capelli d'angelo (angel hair) pasta
1 tablespoon (15 ml) olive oil
1 cup (140 g) cooked, shredded ham
¾ cup (55 g) fresh sliced mushrooms
1 roasted red capsicum, chopped
2 tablespoons (30 ml) flour
1 340-g (12-ounce) can evaporated milk
1 cup (110 g) shredded Swiss cheese

- Preheat oven at 205° C (400° F).

- Cook pasta in saucepan according to package directions, drain and set aside.

- Heat oil in large frypan over medium heat and cook ham and mushrooms for 4 minutes or until mushrooms are tender. Stir in roasted red capsicum and flour and cook 1 minute.

- Gradually add evaporated milk and a little salt and pepper; cook over medium heat, stirring constantly, until it thickens. Stir in ham-mushroom mixture, pasta and ½ cup (55 g) cheese.

- Spoon evenly into sprayed 23-cm (9-inch) pie pan and sprinkle with remaining cheese.

- Bake for 15 minutes. Let stand for 5 minutes before cutting into wedges to serve. Serves 6.

Prime Time Mac 'n Ham

340 g (12 ounces) rotelle
    (wagon wheels) pasta
280 g (10 ounces) frozen green peas,
    thawed
1 cup (250 ml) milk
2 230-g (8-ounce) packets cream
    cheese
¾ cup (30 g) shredded cheddar
    cheese
2 cups (280 g) cooked, cubed ham
1 230-g (8-ounce) can whole corn
    kernels, drained

- Cook pasta in large saucepan
  according to package directions and
  stir in peas last minute of cooking
  time. Drain pasta and peas and
  return to saucepan.

- Place milk, cream cheese and
  cheddar cheese in medium
  saucepan on medium heat. Heat and
  stir until cheese melts and mixture
  is smooth.

- Add ham and corn, mix well and
  heat until mixture is thoroughly
  hot. Fold into cooked pasta and
  place in serving bowl. Serves 8.

Ravioli-Ham Dinner

510 g (18 ounces) refrigerated
    cheese-filled ravioli pasta
1 740-g (26-ounce) jar tomato
    pasta sauce
1 115-g (4-ounce) can sliced
    mushrooms
1 tablespoon (15 ml) dried onion
    flakes
1 cup (140 g) cooked, chopped
    ham
1½ cups (175 g) shredded
    mozzarella cheese

- Cook pasta according to package
  directions; drain and cover to
  keep warm.

- Combine pasta sauce, mushrooms,
  onion flakes and ham in saucepan
  and mix well. Bring mixture to a
  boil, reduce heat and simmer for
  10 minutes or until sauce is slightly
  thick, stirring frequently.

- Stir in pasta and stir gently
  to coat. Spoon into serving
  platter and sprinkle with cheese.
  Serves 6 to 8.

Rich Fettuccini

¼ cup (60 g) butter
2 teaspoons (10 ml) minced garlic
230 g (8 ounces) fresh mushrooms,
    sliced
1 small red capsicum,
    seeded, chopped
2 teaspoons dried basil
2 teaspoons dried oregano
½ teaspoon cayenne pepper
2 cups (280 g) cooked, chopped
    ham
500 ml (1 pint) pouring cream
1 cup (250 g) spaghetti sauce
455 g (16 ounces) fettuccini (medium
    egg noodles) pasta
Parmesan cheese

- Melt butter in large saucepan on medium heat and cook garlic, mushrooms and capsicum for about 5 minutes, stirring often. Add in basil, oregano, cayenne pepper, ham and a little salt and cook for additional 5 minutes.

- Pour in cream and bring to a boil and slowly stir in spaghetti sauce, stirring often. Reduce heat to medium and stir until sauce reduces by one-third and begins to thicken.

- Cook pasta in saucepan according to package directions, drain and transfer to serving bowl. Ladle sauce over pasta and serve hot. Sprinkle parmesan cheese over top. Serves 8.

Spinach with Pasta

255 g (9 ounces) fresh spinach
280 g (10 ounces) frozen,
    sliced yellow squash
230 g (8 ounces) refrigerated
    wholemeal fettuccini (medium
    egg noodles) pasta
2 tablespoons (30 ml) olive oil
1 small onion, finely chopped
1 tablespoon (15 ml) flour
1 tablespoon (15 ml) sugar
1 cup (250 ml) chicken stock
2 tablespoons (30 ml) red wine
    vinegar
340 g (¾ pound) deli ham, cut
    into strips

- Bring 1 cup (250 ml) water to a boil in large saucepan and cook spinach and squash for about 5 minutes; drain and keep warm.

- Cook pasta in saucepan according to package directions and drain. Transfer to serving platter and keep warm.

- Heat oil in large frypan and sauté onion until tender. Stir in flour, sugar and a little salt and pepper. Quickly stir in stock and vinegar, cook on medium heat and stir until mixture thickens.

- Stir in ham and spinach-squash mixture and mix well. Spoon over pasta and serve immediately. Serves 8.

Tortellini-Ham Dinner

510 g (9 ounces) fresh tortellini pasta
280 g (10 ounces) frozen green peas, thawed
1 455-g (16-ounce) jar alfredo sauce
2–3 cups (280–420 g) cooked, cubed ham

- Cook pasta in saucepan according to package directions. Add green peas for about 5 minutes before pasta is done. Drain.

- Heat alfredo sauce and ham in saucepan until thoroughly hot. Toss with pasta and peas. Serves 8 to 10.

Carbonara Frypan Pie

230 g (8 ounces) spaghetti pasta
8 slices bacon, chopped
3 eggs
1 455-g (16-ounce) jar alfredo sauce
½ cup (50 g) grated parmesan cheese
1 230-g (8-ounce) can green peas, drained

- Cook pasta in saucepan according to package directions and drain. Cook bacon in frypan on medium-high heat until crisp and drain. Discard bacon drippings.

- Whisk eggs, 1 cup (250 ml) alfredo sauce and cheese in large bowl. Stir in pasta, peas and chopped bacon and place in same frypan used to cook bacon. Cook over medium heat for about 5 minutes or until bottom is slightly crisp.

- Spoon remaining sauce over top, cover and cook for 7 to 8 minutes. Cut in wedges to serve. Serves 5 to 6.

Carbonara sauce is a relatively modern invention dating from World War II when American soldiers in Italy asked for bacon and eggs. The sauce is made with bacon, eggs and cream.

Cheesy Fettuccini and Bacon

455 g (16 ounces) fettuccini (medium
   egg noodles) pasta
230 g (8 ounces) precooked bacon
3 large eggs
⅔ cup (70 g) grated parmesan
   cheese
1½ cups (470 g) unthickened
   cream
1 230-g (8-ounce) can baby green
   peas, drained

- Cook pasta in saucepan according
  to package directions and drain.
  Cut bacon into 1.2-cm (½-inch)
  pieces with scissors.

- Beat eggs, cheese, cream, peas and
  a little salt and pepper in bowl.
  Pour egg mixture and bacon pieces
  over pasta and gently toss with
  tongs.

- Return pasta mixture to pan on low
  heat and cook, stirring constantly
  for about 2 to 3 minutes or until it
  thickens slightly. (Do not overcook
  or eggs will scramble.) Serves 8.

Pork 'n Pasta

455 g (1 pound) pork tenderloin,
   cut into (1.2-cm) ½-inch
   pieces
280 g (10 ounces) frozen mixed
   vegetables
½ cup rotini (spiral) pasta, cooked
¼ teaspoon cayenne pepper
1 425-g (15-ounce) can cannellini
   beans, drained
3 roma tomatoes, seeded, chopped
1 cup (250 ml) alfredo sauce
⅓ cup (35 g) grated parmesan
   cheese

- Cook pork in large frypan on
  medium-high for 10 minutes,
  stirring frequently.

- Stir in vegetables, pasta and
  cayenne pepper; mix well. Reduce
  heat to medium; cover and cook for
  7 to 8 minutes or until vegetables
  are tender but crisp, stirring
  occasionally.

- Stir in beans, tomatoes and alfredo
  sauce and cook until mixture is
  thoroughly hot. Place in serving
  bowl and sprinkle with parmesan
  cheese. Serves 8.

Sensational Spaghetti

Forget the tomato sauce.
This is spaghetti to love!

½ cup (115 g) butter
1½ teaspoons minced garlic
340 g (12 ounces) vermicelli (thin spaghetti) pasta
1 cup (100 g) grated parmesan cheese
455 g (1 pint) pouring cream
1 teaspoon dried parsley flakes
10–12 slices bacon, fried crisp, crumbled

- Preheat oven to 160° C (325° F).

- Melt butter in large frypan and sauté garlic until slightly brown. Cook pasta in saucepan according to package directions and drain.

- Combine garlic mixture, pasta, parmesan cheese, cream, parsley flakes, and ½ teaspoon each of salt and pepper in bowl and mix well.

- Spoon into sprayed 2-L (2-quart) baking dish. Cover and bake just until warm, for about 15 minutes.

- Uncover and sprinkle crumbled bacon over casserole.
  Serves 6 to 8.

Oodles
of Noodles

680–910 g (1½–2 pounds) pork
    tenderloin
3 tablespoons (45 ml) olive oil
2 sticks celery, chopped
1 green and 1 red capsicum,
    seeded, chopped
1 onion, chopped
1 115-g (4-ounce) can sliced
    mushrooms
1 280-g (10-ounce) can tomatoes
2 green chillies, chopped
1 280-g (10-ounce) can cream
    of mushroom soup
1 teaspoon minced garlic
1 280-g (10-ounce) can cream
    of celery soup
¼ cup (60 ml) soy sauce
200 g (7 ounces) elbow macaroni
    (tube) pasta, cooked, drained
2 cups (110 g) chow mein noodles

- Preheat oven to 175° C (350° F).

- Cut pork into 2.5-cm (1-inch) cubes. Brown pork in oil in frypan and cook on low heat for about 15 minutes. Remove pork with slotted spoon to side dish.

- Sauté celery, capsicums and onion in same frypan in remaining oil. Combine pork, celery-onion mixture, mushrooms, tomatoes, green chillies, soups, soy sauce and pasta in large bowl.

- Spoon casserole into 1 sprayed 23 x 33-cm (9 x 13-inch) baking dish or 2 smaller baking dishes. Top with chow mein noodles.

- Bake for 50 minutes. Serves 10.

TIP: *If you make 2 smaller casseroles, you can freeze one. Wait to sprinkle the chow mein noodles over casserole until just before you place it in the oven to cook.*

Pork-Fettuccini Supreme

Olive oil
910 g (2 pounds) pork
    tenderloin, cut
    into 2.5-cm (1-inch) cubes
2 sticks celery, chopped
1 red and 1 green capsicum, seeded,
    chopped
1 onion, chopped
340 g (12 ounces) fettuccini (medium
    egg noodles) pasta,
    cooked, drained
1 280-g (10-ounce) can cream
    of celery soup
1 280-g (10-ounce) can cream
    of chicken soup
1 425-g (15-ounce) can creamed
    corn
¾ cup (235 g) unthickened cream
1½ cups (45 g) cornflakes, crushed
3 tablespoons (45 g) butter, melted

- Preheat oven to 175° C (350° F).

- Heat a little oil in frypan, brown and cook pork for about 15 minutes. Spoon pork into large bowl.

- With a little oil in frypan, sauté celery, capsicum and onion. Spoon into bowl with pork. Add noodles, soups, creamed corn, cream, and a little salt and pepper to pork.

- Mix well and pour into sprayed 23 x 33-cm (9 x 13-inch) baking dish.

- Combine crushed cornflakes and butter in bowl and sprinkle over casserole. Cover and bake for about 30 minutes. Serves 8.

Dinner Ready Stir-Fry

2 tablespoons (30 ml) olive oil
455 g (16 ounces) frozen
    stir-fry vegetables
455 g (1 pound) pork tenderloin,
    cut in strips
2½ teaspoons Cajun seasoning
½ cup (125 ml) prepared peanut
    sauce
1 teaspoon light soy sauce
340 g (12 ounces) vermicelli (thin
    spaghetti) pasta
2 tablespoons (30 g) butter
½ cup (85 g) peanuts, chopped

- Heat oil in wok (or frypan) over medium-high heat and add stir-fry vegetables. Cook and stir for 6 to 8 minutes or until vegetables are tender but crisp. Remove from wok.

- In same wok, toss pork with seasoning. Add more oil if needed. Cook and stir for about 5 minutes or until pork is no longer pink. Add peanut sauce and soy sauce and return vegetables and cook just until thoroughly hot.

- Cook pasta in saucepan according to package directions and drain. Place in hot serving bowl, add butter and stir until butter melts. Spoon pork-vegetable mixture over pasta and top with peanuts. Serves 8.

Tasty Noodles and Pork

680 g (1½ pounds) pork
tenderloin, cubed
Olive oil
2 cups (200 g) celery, chopped
2 cups (320 g) onion, chopped
1 green capsicum,
seeded, chopped
1 red capsicum,
seeded, chopped
1 425-g (15-ounce) can stewed
tomatoes
1 teaspoon paprika
2 280-g (10-ounce) cans
mushroom soup
¼ cup (60 ml) soy sauce
1½ cups (160 g) elbow macaroni
(tube) pasta, cooked, drained
2 cups (110 g) chow mein noodles

- Preheat oven to 175° C (350° F).

- Brown pork in frypan with a little oil and cook on low heat for 15 minutes. Transfer pork with slotted spoon to side dish.

- In same frypan, sauté celery, onion and capsicums.

- Combine pork, celery-capsicum mixture, stewed tomatoes, paprika, mushroom soup, soy sauce and pasta in large bowl.

- Spoon into sprayed 23 x 33-cm (9 x 13-inch) baking dish. Sprinkle noodles on top of casserole and bake for 40 minutes. Serves 8.

Tenderloin, Pasta and Peas

680 g (1½ pounds) pork tenderloin, cubed
Olive oil
1 cup (160 g) onion, chopped
1 cup (100 g) celery, chopped
2 red capsicums, seeded, chopped
230 g (8 ounces) linguine (thin egg noodles) pasta, cooked
1 280-g (10-ounce) can cream of chicken soup
½ cup (40 g) pouring cream
280 g (10 ounces) frozen green peas, thawed
1½ cups (180 g) seasoned breadcrumbs
½ cup (65 g) walnuts, chopped

- Preheat oven to 175° C (350° F).

- Brown pork tenderloin in large frypan with a little oil. Reduce heat and cook for 20 minutes. Remove pork to separate plate.

- In same frypan, sauté onions, celery and capsicums. Add pork, pasta, soup, cream, peas and a little salt and pepper.

- Spoon into sprayed 4-L (4-quart) baking dish and sprinkle with breadcrumbs and walnuts. Bake for 30 minutes or until casserole bubbles around edges. Serves 8.

Best Bubbling Pasta

455 g (16 ounces) fusilli (spiral)
    pasta
455 g (1 pound) Italian sausages
2 425-g (15-ounce) jars tomato
    pasta sauce
1 teaspoon dried basil
425 g (15 ounces) ricotta cheese
2 teaspoons Italian seasoning
455 g (16 ounces) shredded
    mozzarella cheese

- Preheat oven to 175° C (350° F).

- Cook pasta in saucepan according to package directions and drain. Remove casing on sausage and cook in large frypan over medium-high heat until evenly brown; drain and crumble. Set aside. In separate saucepan, place pasta sauce and heat with basil.

- Combine ricotta with 1 teaspoon (5 ml) Italian seasoning and a little salt and pepper in medium bowl.

- Spread about 1 cup (250 ml) pasta sauce in sprayed 23 x 33-cm (9 x 13-inch) baking dish. Layer half pasta, half sausage, half ricotta and half mozzarella cheese.

- Spoon half remaining sauce over top and repeat layers. Sprinkle top with remaining Italian seasoning. Bake for 35 to 40 minutes or until bubbly around edges. Serves 6 to 8.

Colourful Sausage Dinner

455 g (1 pound) cooked Polish
   sausages, cut into
   6-mm (¼-inch) slices
1 red capsicum,
   seeded, julienned
3 small zucchini, sliced
3 small yellow squash, sliced
¼ cup (60 ml) olive oil, divided
455 g (16 ounces) penne (tube) pasta
1 740-g (26-ounce) jar spaghetti
   sauce, heated

- Sauté sausage, capsicum, zucchini and squash with 2 tablespoons (30 ml) oil in large frypan until vegetables are tender but crisp. Keep warm.

- Cook pasta in saucepan according to package directions, drain and stir in remaining oil. Add a little salt and pepper.

- Spoon into large serving bowl and spread hot spaghetti sauce over pasta.

- Use slotted spoon to top with sausage-vegetable mixture and serve immediately. Serve with hot, buttered garlic bread. Serves 8.

Pasta has been a very popular food from its beginning, but it was not served on the tables of the rich and famous because it was eaten with the hands. Then a member of the Spanish court of King Ferdinand II in the 1400s invented the fork especially for eating pasta and history was made.

Creamy Fettuccini

230 g (8 ounces) fettuccini (medium egg noodles) pasta
455 g (1 pound) Italian sausages
1 280-g (10-ounce) can cream of mushroom soup
455 g (16 ounces) sour cream

- Preheat oven to 160° C (325° F).

- Cook pasta in saucepan and drain.

- Cut sausages into 2.5-cm (1-inch) pieces, brown in frypan over medium heat and cook for about 8 minutes. Drain.

- Mix all ingredients in bowl and place in sprayed 2-L (2-quart) baking dish.

- Bake for 30 minutes. Serves 4.

Ideal Linguine and Sausage

2 tablespoons (30 ml) olive oil
455 g (1 pound) Polish sausages, cut in 1.2-cm (½-inch) pieces
1 red capsicum, seeded, chopped
1 115-g (4-ounce) can sliced mushrooms, drained
1 115-g (4-ounce) can sliced black olives
½ teaspoon dried oregano
340 g (12 ounces) linguine (thin egg noodles) pasta
½ cup (125 g) pesto
½ cup (50 g) grated parmesan cheese
4 spring onions, sliced

- Heat oil in large frypan on medium-high and cook sausage and capsicum for about 8 minutes. Stir in mushrooms, olives and oregano and mix well.

- Cook pasta in saucepan according to package directions, drain and stir in pesto and parmesan cheese. Toss until they blend well. Garnish with sliced spring onions. Serves 6.

Italian Sausage-Tortellini

230 g (½ pound) minced steak
455 g (1 pound) bulk
   Italian sausage meat
1 425-g (15-ounce) bottle
   tomato pasta sauce
1 425-g (15-ounce) can Italian
   stewed tomatoes with liquid
1½ cups (105 g) sliced fresh
   mushrooms
255 g (9 ounces) refrigerated cheese-
   filled tortellini pasta
1½ cups (175 g) shredded
   mozzarella cheese

- Brown and cook beef and sausage in large frypan for about 10 minutes on medium-low heat and drain.

- Combine meat mixture, tomato sauce, tomatoes and mushrooms in 4 to 5-L (4 to 5-quart) slow cooker.

- Cover and cook on low for 6 to 8 hours.

- Stir in pasta and sprinkle with mozzarella cheese.

- Turn cooker to high and continue cooking for additional 10 to 15 minutes or until pasta is tender. Serves 4 to 6.

Knock Out Hot Sausage Pasta

3 tablespoons (45 ml) olive oil
455 g (1 pound) hot Italian sausages
1 tablespoon (15 ml) minced garlic
1 red and 1 green capsicum, seeded,
     cut in strips
227 g (8 ounces) mushrooms, sliced
2 eggs at room temperature,
     separated
⅓ cup (80 ml) whipped cream
¾ cup (180 ml) grated romano
     cheese
455 g (16 ounces) vermicelli
     (thin spaghetti) pasta
1 teaspoon dried parsley

- Heat oil in frypan and sauté sausage, garlic, capsicums and mushrooms for about 10 minutes or until sausage is cooked.

- Beat egg yolks and egg whites separately. Gently stir beaten eggs and whipped cream, season with salt and pepper and fold in cheese.

- Cook pasta in saucepan according to package directions, drain and rinse in hot water. Drain again. Transfer pasta to large, hot serving bowl and pour egg-cheese mixture over pasta. Toss until mixture coats pasta well.

- Stir in sausage-mushroom mixture and parsley and toss again. Serve immediately. Serves 6 to 8.

Layered Sausage and Rigatoni

255 g (9 ounces) refrigerated
  rigatoni (large tubes) pasta
455 g (1 pound) bulk Italian pork
  sausage meat
1 795-g (28-ounce) can diced
  tomatoes with liquid
2 teaspoons dried basil leaves
2 teaspoons minced garlic
145 g (5 ounces) grated parmesan
  cheese
1 jar roasted red capsicums,
  chopped
230 g (8 ounces) shredded
  mozzarella cheese

- Preheat oven to 190° C (375° F).

- Cook pasta according to package directions; drain but keep warm.

- Cook sausage in large frypan over medium heat for about 10 minutes, stirring often and until no longer pink; drain.

- Combine tomatoes, basil and garlic in bowl. Layer half each of pasta, sausage, tomato-garlic mixture, parmesan cheese, roasted red capsicums and mozzarella cheese in sprayed 23 x 33-cm (9 x 13-inch) baking dish. Repeat layers.

- Bake for 35 to 45 minutes or until bubbly hot and cheese is golden brown. Serves 8.

The more complex the shape of a pasta, the better a sauce or seasoning will cling to its ridges and grooves, nooks and crannies.

Outstanding Sausage and Broccoli

340 g (12 ounces) farfalle
(bow-tie) pasta
280 g (10 ounces) frozen
broccoli florets
2 tablespoons (30 ml) olive oil
455 g (1 pound) Polish sausages,
cut into 6-mm (¼-inch) slices
2 teaspoons minced garlic
1 red capsicum, seeded,
julienned
1 tablespoon (15 ml) flour
¼ teaspoon red pepper flakes
1½ cups (375 ml) chicken stock
2 tablespoons (30 ml) balsamic
vinegar

- Cook pasta in large saucepan according to package directions, but add broccoli for last 5 minutes of cooking time. Drain immediately and return pasta and broccoli to warm pan.

- Heat oil in large frypan and cook sausage, garlic and capsicum for 5 to 6 minutes. Stir in flour, red pepper and a little salt. Add stock and vinegar. Cook, stirring often, for 2 minutes.

- On medium-low heat, pour sausage-stock mixture over pasta and toss. Heat thoroughly and serve immediately. Serves 8 to 10.

Salami Twirls

2 cups (210 g) tri-colour
    twirls pasta
455 g (1 pound) bulk Italian
    sausage meat
1 onion, chopped
1 green capsicum,
    seeded, chopped
1 425-g (15-ounce) jar pasta sauce
1 230-g (8-ounce) can tomato
    soup
⅓ cup (75 ml) milk
85 g (3 ounces) sliced salami, halved
1 115-g (4-ounce) jar sliced
    mushrooms, drained
1 600-g (2-ounce) can sliced black
    olives, drained
230 g (8 ounces) shredded
    mozzarella cheese

- Preheat oven to 175° C (350° F).

- Cook pasta twirls in saucepan according to package directions and drain.

- Cook sausage, onion and capsicum in frypan over medium heat until sausage is no longer pink and drain.

- Combine pasta sauce, tomato soup and milk in large bowl. Stir in sausage mixture, pasta twirls, salami, mushrooms, olives and half cheese and mix well.

- Spoon into sprayed 23 x 33-cm (9 x 13-inch) baking dish. Cover and bake for 30 minutes.

- Remove from oven and sprinkle remaining cheese over top of casserole and return to oven for 5 to 10 minutes or just until cheese is melted. Serves 8.

Proud Italian Spaghetti

455 g (1 pound) Italian sausages,
    chopped
1 green capsicum, seeded,
    coarsely chopped
1 onion, chopped
1 740-g (26-ounce) can spaghetti
    sauce with mushrooms
1 280-g (10-ounce) can tomatoes
2 chopped green chillies
340 g (12 ounces) spaghetti pasta
230 g (8 ounces) shredded
    mozzarella cheese

- Lightly brown sausages in large
  frypan on medium heat. Add
  capsicum and onion and cook
  until soft, but not brown. Stir in
  spaghetti sauce, tomatoes and green
  chillies. Reduce heat to medium-
  low and simmer for about
  15 minutes.

- Cook pasta in saucepan according
  to package directions, drain and
  place on serving platter. Spoon
  sausage-tomato sauce mixture over
  pasta and sprinkle cheese over top.
  Serves 4 to 5.

Ravioli and Tomatoes

255 g (9 ounces) refrigerated
    sausage-filled ravioli pasta
1 425-g (15-ounce) can
    stewed tomatoes
2 115-g (4-ounce) cans sliced
    mushrooms
145 g (5 ounces) grated parmesan
    cheese

- Cook pasta in saucepan according
  to package directions and drain
  well. Stir in stewed tomatoes and
  mushrooms and bring to a boil.
  Reduce heat to low and simmer for
  about 5 minutes.

- Transfer to serving dish and
  sprinkle cheese on each serving.
  Serves 6.

Zesty Ziti

455 g (1 pound) Italian sausages,
    cut into 1.2-cm (½-inch) pieces
1 onion, coarsely chopped
1 green capsicum, seeded, sliced
Olive oil
1 425-g (15-ounce) can diced
    tomatoes
1 425-g (15-ounce) can Italian
    stewed tomatoes
2 tablespoons (35 g) tomato sauce
455 g (16 ounces) ziti (thin tubes)
    pasta
1 cup (115 g) shredded mozzarella
    cheese

- Preheat oven to 175° C (350° F).

- Cook sausage, onion and capsicum in a little oil in large frypan over medium heat and drain.

- Add diced tomatoes, stewed tomatoes and tomato soup and mix well.

- Cook pasta in saucepan according to package directions and drain.

- Combine sausage-tomato mixture in large bowl and toss with pasta and cheese.

- Spoon into sprayed 3-L (3-quart) baking dish. Cover and bake for 20 minutes. Serves 8.

Pasta
with Seafood

*Gifts from the sea are enhanced
with pasta in these delectable
recipes. The texture and variety
make menu selection easy.*

Pasta with Seafood Contents

If you want to make pasta ahead of time, cook as usual; be sure not to overcook. Drain and rinse under cold running water to stop the cooking process. Drain completely and cool. Toss with a small amount of oil (just a couple of teaspoons unless you have a large amount of pasta) so it will not stick together. It can be refrigerated for up to 3 days. Do not freeze.

Fettuccini of the Sea

¼ cup (60 g) butter
¼ cup (30 g) flour
1 teaspoon Cajun seasoning
1 tablespoon (15 ml) minced garlic
455 g (16 ounces) unthickened cream
½ cup (125 ml) milk
½ cup (75 g) red capsicum, seeded, finely chopped
2 170-g (6-ounce) cans prawns, peeled veined
2 170-g (6-ounce) cans crabmeat, drained, flaked
1 170-g (6-ounce) can chopped clams, drained
½ cup (50 g) grated parmesan cheese
340 g (12 ounces) fettuccini (medium egg noodles) pasta, cooked al dente

- Preheat oven to 160° C (325° F).

- Melt butter in saucepan and add flour, Cajun seasoning, ¾ teaspoon (4 ml) pepper and garlic and mix well. Gradually add cream and milk and mix well. Cook on medium heat, stirring constantly, until it thickens.

- Add capsicum, prawns, crabmeat, clams and parmesan cheese and heat thoroughly.

- Spoon half pasta and half seafood sauce in sprayed 23 x 33-cm (9 x 13-inch) baking dish. Repeat layers.

- Cover and bake for 25 minutes or just until casserole bubbles. Serves 8.

Flavours that Thai

230 g (8 ounces) vermicelli (thin spaghetti) pasta
1 cup (100 g) fresh snowpeas
1 tablespoon (15 ml) olive oil
230 g (8 ounces) sliced mushrooms
1 stick celery, finely sliced
455 g (16 ounces) shredded carrots
230 g (8 ounces) imitation crabmeat
1 230-g (8-ounce) jar Thai peanut sauce
½ teaspoon hot chilli sauce
2 teaspoons toasted sesame seeds

- Cook pasta in saucepan according to package directions and add snowpeas last 2 minutes of cooking time. Set aside and keep warm.

- Heat oil in large frypan over medium-high heat and add mushrooms, celery and carrots. Cook and stir for 3 minutes or until celery and carrots are tender.

- Add crabmeat, cook and stir until mixture is thoroughly hot. Add peanut sauce and hot chilli sauce. Cook and stir until mixture is thoroughly hot.

- Drain pasta and snowpeas well and place into serving bowl. Spoon crab-peanut sauce mixture over pasta mixture and top with sesame seeds. Serves 4.

Florentine Prawns and Pasta

510 g (18 ounces) frozen, thawed creamed spinach
340 g (12 ounces) penne (tube) pasta
¼ cup (20 g) pouring cream
1 teaspoon Cajun seasoning
455 g (1 pound) peeled, medium prawns
2 tablespoons (30 ml) olive oil

- Heat spinach in saucepan.

- In separate large saucepan, cook pasta according to package directions. Drain, add cream and Cajun seasoning and mix until they blend well.

- Cook prawns in frypan with olive oil for about 3 minutes or until thoroughly cooked (but not over-cooked).

- Add spinach to pasta. Stir in prawns and transfer to serving dish. Serves 6.

Penne pasta is a tubular pasta with ridges and is cut diagonally at both ends. Its name means 'pens' in Italian because of the shape, like the point of a quill pen. It is also known as penne rigate *because of the ridges. If it is smooth, it's called* penne lisce.

Marinara and Veggies

230 g (8 ounces) vermicelli (thin spaghetti) pasta
2 tablespoons (30 ml) olive oil
1 teaspoon minced garlic
½ cup (80 g) chopped onion
1 medium zucchini, sliced
2 small yellow squash, sliced
455 g (16 ounces) imitation crabmeat
230 g (8 ounces) tomato pasta sauce, heated
2 tablespoons (10 g) fresh chopped parsley

- Cook pasta according to package directions and drain.

- Heat oil in large frypan and cook garlic and onion for about 3 minutes or until onion is tender but crisp.

- Stir in zucchini, squash and a little salt and pepper. Cook for 2 to 3 minutes or until squash is tender; remove squash from frypan.

- Place crabmeat in frypan and cook on medium heat for 2 minutes, stirring often.

- Spoon pasta into serving bowl; spoon half pasta sauce and top with vegetables and crabmeat. Drizzle with remaining pasta sauce and sprinkle with parsley. Serves 8.

Lasagna-Tomato Toss

455 g (16 ounces) lasagna sheets
1 onion, chopped
1 tablespoon (15 ml) olive oil
1 795-g (28-ounce) can diced
    tomatoes
¼ teaspoon cayenne pepper
¾ teaspoon dried oregano
455 g (16 ounces) imitation
    crabmeat
2 teaspoons (10 ml) dried parsley
¾ cup (100 g) crumbled feta cheese

- Break lasagna sheets in half and cook in saucepan according to package directions, but add 2 minutes to cooking time. Drain later.

- Cook onion with oil in frypan for about 6 minutes and stir in tomatoes, cayenne pepper and oregano. Heat to boiling and break up tomatoes with side of spoon.

- Reduce heat to medium and cook for about 8 minutes to thicken slightly. Stir in crabmeat and cook until thoroughly hot.

- Drain pasta and return to saucepan. Add crabmeat mixture, parsley and ½ cup (70 g) feta cheese to pasta in saucepan and toss to coat well. Sprinkle with remaining feta cheese. Serves 4 to 6.

Drain cooked pasta but do not rinse it unless the recipe calls for this process. Usually, pasta is rinsed for use in salads. It's also a good idea to rinse lasagna sheets so they do not stick together.

Seafood Lasagna

8 lasagna sheets
2 tablespoons (30 g) butter
1 onion, chopped
230 g (8 ounces) cream cheese,
    softened
425 g (15 ounces) ricotta cheese
1 roasted red capsicum, chopped
1 egg, beaten
2 teaspoons dried basil
2 280-g (10-ounce) cans cream
    of celery soup
1 fish stock cube
¼ cup (60 ml) milk
⅓ cup (75 ml) white wine
455 g (1 pound) small, cooked
    prawns, peeled, veined
2 170-g (6-ounce) cans crabmeat,
    drained, flaked
¼ cup (25 g) grated parmesan
    cheese
1 cup (115 g) shredded cheddar
    cheese

- Preheat oven to 175° C (350° F).

- Cook lasagna sheets in saucepan according to package directions and set aside.

- Melt butter in frypan and sauté onion until tender, but do not brown. Stir in cream cheese, ricotta cheese, roasted red capsicum, egg, basil, ½ teaspoon each of salt and pepper.

- Combine soups, stock cube, milk and wine in saucepan and heat just to mix well. Add prawns and crabmeat.

- Layer four lasagna sheets in sprayed 23 x 33-cm (9 x 13-inch) baking dish.

- Spread half of cream cheese-roasted red capsicum mixture over pasta and top with half seafood mixture. Repeat layers with remaining four lasagna sheets, cream cheese-roasted red capsicum mixture, then seafood mixture.

- Sprinkle with parmesan cheese and bake for 45 minutes.

- Remove from oven, top with cheddar cheese and return to oven for 3 to 4 minutes or just until cheese melts. Serves 8 to 10.

Crabmeat and Pasta Alfredo

230 g (8 ounces) farfalle (bow-tie) pasta
2 slices bacon, cut into 1.2-cm (½-inch) pieces
2 sticks celery, sliced
285 g (10 ounces) frozen green peas
455 g (16 ounces) imitation crabmeat
1 cup (245 g) alfredo sauce
2 tablespoons (6 g) fresh chives, chopped

- Cook pasta according to package directions, drain and set aside.

- Cook bacon in large frypan on medium heat for about 5 minutes or until crisp. Stir in celery, green peas and add ¼ cup water; cover and cook for 2 minutes, stirring often, until water has evaporated.

- Add crabmeat and cook for 3 minutes. Stir in alfredo sauce and pasta and cook over medium-low heat, stirring gently until thoroughly hot. Sprinkle with chives. Serves 8.

Alfredo sauce is made with cheese and butter. It is named for the Roman chef who created it.

Crab Florentine

1 tablespoon (15 ml) olive oil
1½ cups (155 g) orzo (tiny) pasta
1 red capsicum, seeded, chopped
3 spring onions, chopped
1 teaspoon minced garlic
½ teaspoon dried dill
½ litre (14 ounces) chicken stock
1 teaspoon lemon juice
2 cups (60 g) shredded spinach
455 g (16 ounces) imitation
    crabmeat
⅓ cup (35 g) grated parmesan
    cheese

- Heat oil in large frypan on medium-high heat and cook pasta, capsicum, onions and garlic for 3 to 4 minutes or until vegetables are tender but crisp.

- Stir in dill, stock, lemon juice and 1 cup (250 ml) water. Heat to boiling; reduce heat. Cover and simmer for about 10 minutes or until pasta is tender.

- Stir in spinach and crabmeat and cook for 2 to 3 minutes. Spoon into serving bowl and sprinkle parmesan cheese over top. Serves 8.

The name of the tiny, rice-shaped pasta known as 'orzo' means 'barley'.

Simply Delicious

¼ cup (60 ml) olive oil
1 tablespoon (15 ml) minced
    garlic
1 yellow capsicum, seeded,
    cut into thin strips
3 425-g (15-ounce) cans Italian
    stewed tomatoes with liquid
1½ teaspoons Italian seasoning
¾ cup (55 g) pouring cream
455 g (16 ounces) imitation
    crabmeat
½ teaspoon chilli flakes
455 g (16 ounces) spinach linguine
    (thin egg noodles) pasta
1½ cups (105 g) fresh broccoli
    florets
½ cup (50 g) grated parmesan
    cheese

- Heat oil in large, deep frypan and sauté garlic and capsicum for 5 minutes.

- Drain stewed tomatoes and save liquid. Add Italian seasoning and puree in blender or food processor. Add pureed mixture and liquid to frypan and bring to a boil. Reduce heat to medium and cook for 25 minutes or until mixture thickens.

- Stir cream, crabmeat and chilli into frypan with tomato mixture and heat thoroughly over medium heat, stirring occasionally.

- Cook pasta in saucepan according to package directions, except add broccoli last 4 minutes of cooking time. Drain and place onto hot serving platter. Spoon crab sauce over pasta-broccoli mixture and top with parmesan cheese to serve. Serves 6 to 8.

Simple Crab and Asparagus

455 g (16 ounces) imitation
    crabmeat
1 bunch fresh asparagus spears
230 g (8 ounces) fusilli
    (spiral) pasta
2 tablespoons (15 g) flour
½ cup (120 g) sour cream
1½ cups (375 ml) chicken stock
1 tablespoon (15 ml) lemon juice
¼ teaspoon white pepper

- Cut asparagus spears into 3-cm (1½-inch) pieces. Cook asparagus in ¾ cup (175 ml) boiling water in saucepan for about 8 minutes or until tender but crisp. Drain and reserve ¼ cup (60 ml) liquid.

- Set aside 1 cup (135 g) asparagus pieces, especially tips and keep warm. Puree remaining asparagus with reserved liquid in food processor until nearly smooth.

- Cook pasta in saucepan according to package directions, but add crabmeat last 3 minutes of cooking time. Drain immediately and return pasta and crab to pan and add remaining asparagus pieces.

- Combine flour and sour cream in medium saucepan and mix well. Over medium heat, add stock, lemon juice, white pepper and a little salt. Stir and cook until mixture thickens; cook and stir for additional 1 minute. Pour stock mixture over pasta mixture, toss and serve immediately. Serves 6 to 8.

Spiced Prawns Over Pasta

230 g (8 ounces) ziti (thin tubes) pasta
455 g (16 ounces) frozen broccoli florets, thawed, drained
1½ cups (375 ml) chicken stock
2 tablespoons (15 g) cornflour
1 tablespoon (15 ml) Dijon-style mustard
2 tablespoons (30 ml) lemon juice
1 teaspoon chilli flakes
2 tablespoons (30 ml) olive oil
455 g (1 pound) peeled, veined prawns

- Cook pasta in saucepan according to package directions and add broccoli last 5 minutes of cooking time. Drain.

- Stir stock, cornflour, mustard, lemon juice and chilli in small bowl; set aside.

- Heat oil in large frypan over medium-high heat and add prawns; sauté for 1 minute, stirring constantly. Stir stock-cornflour mixture again and stir into frypan with prawns.

- Cook and stir for about 2 minutes or until sauce thickens and bubbles and prawns turn pink. Toss sauce with pasta-broccoli mixture and serve immediately. Serves 4 to 6.

Winner's Circle Crab

455 g (16 ounces) imitation
    crabmeat
1 tablespoon (15 ml) olive oil
1 tablespoon (15 ml) Cajun
    seasoning
230 g (8 ounces) fettuccini (medium
    egg noodles) pasta
2 tablespoons (30 g) butter
460 g (16 ounces) mushrooms, sliced
¼ cup (30 g) finely diced onion
½ litre (14 ounces) chicken stock
½ cup (120 g) sour cream
1 tablespoon (15 ml) cornflour
1 cup (135 g) roasted red
    capsicums, drained, chopped
1 tablespoon (15 ml) capers,
    drained

- Place crabmeat in bowl and add oil and Cajun seasoning; toss to coat.

- Cook pasta in saucepan according to package directions, drain and keep warm.

- Melt butter in large frypan over medium heat, cook mushrooms and onion for about 5 minutes. Remove from pan and stir in crabmeat; set aside.

- In same frypan add ⅔ cup (150 ml) stock and bring to a boil. Cook until reduced to about ¼ cup (60 ml).

- Stir sour cream and cornflour in small bowl. Mix into remaining stock and cook until thick and bubbly.

- Stir in crabmeat, mushroom mixture, roasted red capsicums and capers. Heat just until thoroughly hot. Spoon pasta into serving bowl and spoon crabmeat mixture over pasta. Serves 4 to 6.

Neptune Lasagna

3 tablespoons (45 g) butter
1 red capsicum, seeded, chopped
1 onion, chopped
230 g (8 ounces) cream cheese,
    softened
455 g (16 ounces) cottage cheese
1 egg, beaten
2 teaspoons dried basil
2 teaspoons Cajun seasoning
1 fish stock cube
2 280-g (10-ounce) cans cream
    of celery soup
2 teaspoons dried basil
½ cup (125 ml) white wine
¾ cup (175 ml) milk
460 g (8 ounces) imitation crabmeat
340 g (6 ounces) prawns, rinsed,
    drained
9 lasagna sheets, cooked, drained
85 g (3 ounces) grated parmesan
    cheese
1 cup (115 g) shredded cheddar
    cheese

- Preheat oven to 175° C (350° F).

- Heat butter in frypan and sauté capsicum and onion. Reduce heat and add cream cheese and stir until cream cheese melts.

- Remove from heat and add cottage cheese, egg, basil, ½ teaspoon pepper and Cajun seasoning and set aside.

- Combine both soups, basil, white wine, milk, crabmeat and prawns in bowl and mix well.

- Arrange 3 lasagna sheets in sprayed 23 x 33-cm (9 x 13-inch) baking dish. Spread with one-third of cottage cheese mixture and one-third seafood mixture. Repeat layers twice.

- Sprinkle with parmesan cheese. Cover and bake for about 40 minutes.

- Uncover and sprinkle with cheddar cheese and bake for additional 10 minutes or until lasagna bubbles. Let stand for at least 15 minutes before serving. Serves 9.

Angel Hair and Crab Bake

1 onion, chopped
1 capsicum, seeded, chopped
2 sticks celery, chopped
6 tablespoons (90 g) butter
1 teaspoon dried basil
1 teaspoon parsley flakes
2 425-g (15-ounce) cans Italian
    stewed tomatoes
½ cup (125 ml) dry white wine
455 g (1 pound) crabmeat, flaked
280 g (10 ounces) capelli d'angelo
    (angel hair) pasta, cooked
⅓ cup (35 g) parmesan cheese

- Sauté onion, capsicum and celery in large saucepan with melted butter in large saucepan. Stir in basil, parsley flakes and a little salt and pepper. Add stewed tomatoes and wine. Bring to boil, reduce heat and simmer for 5 minutes.

- Add crabmeat and simmer for 10 minutes. Spread pasta on serving platter and top with crab-mixture. Sprinkle parmesan over crab-mixture. Serves 6.

Before tomatoes were brought to Europe from the Americas, pasta was generally eaten with seasoning or with cheese. Tomatoes revolutionised pasta. Italy had an ideal growing climate for tomatoes. Tomato sauces were popular with pasta by the early 1800s.

Complete Crab Casserole

2 170-g (6-ounce) cans crabmeat, drained
1 280-g (10-ounce) can cream of celery soup
1 chopped roasted red capsicum
¾ cup (175 ml) milk
⅔ cup (150 g) mayonnaise
¾ cup (85 g) shredded cheddar cheese
2 cups (210 g) tagliatelle (thin egg noodles) pasta
½ cup (60 g) seasoned breadcrumbs

- Preheat oven to 175° C (350° F).

- Combine all ingredients except breadcrumbs in large bowl and pour into sprayed 3-L (3-quart) baking dish. Sprinkle breadcrumbs over top of casserole. Cover and bake for 45 minutes. Serves 6 to 8.

Thai Peanuts and Noodles

155 g (5.5 ounces) Thai stir-fry rice noodles
455 g (1 pound) peeled, veined prawns
280 g (10 ounces) frozen broccoli florets, thawed
Olive oil
½ cup (85 g) chopped peanuts

- Bring 3 cups (750 ml) water in saucepan on high heat to a boil and stir in noodles. Turn heat off and let noodles soak for about 5 minutes. Drain and rinse in cold water.

- Sauté prawns and broccoli in frypan with a little oil for about 8 minutes or just until prawns are pink. Add softened noodles, seasoning packet and peanuts. Serves 6.

TIP: *If noodles are still too firm, add 1 tablespoon (15 ml) water and stir-fry until tender.*

Halibut with Orzo

½ cup (125 ml) extra-virgin olive
   oil, divided
¼ cup (60 ml) fresh lemon juice
4 170-g (6-ounce) halibut fillets
455 g (16 ounces) orzo (tiny) pasta
2 teaspoons minced garlic
255 g (9 ounces) baby spinach
1½ cups (225 g) halved cherry
   tomatoes

- Preheat oven to 205° C (400° F).

- Whisk 4 tablespoons (60 ml) olive
  oil and lemon juice in bowl. Place
  halibut on sprayed baking pan
  and sprinkle with a little salt and
  pepper. Drizzle with dressing and
  bake for about 12 minutes or just
  until opaque in centre.

- Cook pasta in saucepan according
  to package directions and drain.
  Add remaining olive oil and garlic
  to same saucepan and sauté over
  medium heat for 1 minute.

- Stir in drained pasta, spinach and
  tomatoes and stir to coat. Season
  with a little salt and pepper.

- Remove from heat, cover and let
  stand for 1 to 2 minutes (spinach
  will wilt). Place pasta mixture on
  serving platter, top with halibut
  fillets and remaining dressing.
  Serves 4.

Celebration Clams and Linguine

340 g (12 ounces) linguine (thin egg noodles) pasta
1½ cups (375 ml) chicken stock
½ onion, finely chopped
2 teaspoons minced garlic
2 170-g (6-ounce) cans chopped clams with liquid
1 tablespoon (15 ml) dried parsley
2 teaspoons lemon juice

- Cook pasta in saucepan according to package directions.

- While pasta cooks, place ½ cup (125 ml) chicken stock, onion and garlic in large saucepan on high heat and bring to a boil. Reduce heat to medium-low and cook for about 5 minutes or until onion is soft.

- Add clam liquid and remaining stock and bring to a boil. Reduce heat to medium and simmer for 4 minutes for flavours to blend. Stir in clams and cook until mixture is thoroughly hot.

- Drain pasta and return to pot; add clam sauce, parsley, lemon juice and a little salt and pepper. Toss to mix well and pour into warmed serving bowl. Serves 6 to 8.

There are at least 350 different shapes and sizes of pasta.

Red Clam Sauce over Vermicelli

1 tablespoon (15 ml) olive oil
1 teaspoon minced garlic
2 200-g (7-ounce) cans chopped
    clams with liquid
1 230-g (8-ounce) can tomato soup
1 teaspoon dried parsley
3 tablespoons (20 g) grated
    parmesan cheese, divided
½ teaspoon dried basil
½ teaspoon dried oregano
Dash of cayenne pepper
230 g (8 ounces) vermicelli
    (thin spaghetti) pasta
1 cup (35 g) bean sprouts

- Place oil in frypan over medium-high heat and sauté garlic for 1 minute. Drain clams and save liquid from 1 can. Set clams aside.

- Add saved liquid, tomato soup, parsley, 1 tablespoon (15 ml) cheese, basil, oregano and cayenne pepper to frypan. Cover and simmer on low heat for 30 minutes. Stir in clams and cook until clam sauce is thoroughly hot.

- Cook pasta in saucepan according to package directions, drain and place in serving bowl. Add bean sprouts and toss. Pour clam sauce over pasta and sprouts and sprinkle with remaining cheese.
Serves 3 to 4.

Spaghetti with Clam Sauce

230 g (8 ounces) vermicelli (thin spaghetti) pasta
1 400-g (14-ounce) can minced clams
2 cups (500 ml) milk
¼ cup (60 g) butter
1 tablespoon (15 ml) chopped onion flakes
1 teaspoon minced garlic
¼ cup (30 g) flour
½ teaspoon dried basil
¼ cup (60 ml) white wine
¼ cup (25 g) grated parmesan cheese

- Cook pasta in saucepan according to package directions, drain and keep warm in serving bowl.

- Drain clams and save liquid. To liquid, add enough milk to equal 1¾ cups (425 ml).

- To make clam sauce, melt butter in saucepan over medium heat. Sauté onion and garlic for 1 minute and stir in flour, basil and a little salt and pepper.

- Add milk mixture and cook, while stirring, until it thickens and bubbles, for about 5 minutes. Stir in wine and clams.

- Spoon sauce over pasta, sprinkle with cheese and serve immediately. Serves 4.

Don't read this if you're eating lunch! Vermicelli is the Italian word for 'little worms'.

Crabmeat Alfredo

4 tablespoons (60 ml) extra-virgin
    olive oil
½ cup (50 g) finely chopped fresh
    spring onions
½ cup (75 g) finely chopped green
    capsicum
2 sticks celery, finely chopped
1 tablespoon (15 ml) minced garlic
1 litre (1 quart) pouring cream
¼ cup (60 g) butter
1 tablespoon (15 ml) Italian
    seasoning
¼ teaspoon cayenne pepper
910 g (2 pounds) imitation crabmeat
230 g (8 ounces) fettuccini (medium
    egg noodles) pasta, cooked
⅔ cup (65 g) grated romano cheese
1 teaspoon dried parsley

- Heat oil in large, heavy soup pot and sauté onions, capsicum, celery and garlic for 3 to 4 minutes. Stir often to keep garlic from burning.

- With heat on high, gradually add in cream, stirring constantly and cook until mixture thickens. Add butter and continue cooking and stirring until sauce thickens to texture of semi-thick paste.

- Add Italian seasoning, cayenne pepper and crabmeat; cook for 3 minutes.

- Add cooked pasta to crabmeat mixture in soup pot and gently fold all ingredients. Stir in cheese, parsley and a little salt. With soup pot on low, heat just until mixture is thoroughly hot. Serve piping hot. Serves 8 to 10.

Fettuccini a la Crabmeat

340 g (12 ounces) fettuccini (medium egg noodles) pasta
3 capsicums, seeded, chopped
3 onions, chopped
6 sticks celery, chopped
1½ cups (345 g) butter
400 g (14 ounces) imitation crabmeat
2 tablespoons (30 ml) snipped parsley
4–5 cloves garlic, minced
500 ml (1 pint) carton unthickened cream
½ cup (60 g) flour
455 g (16 ounces) cubed cheddar cheese

- Preheat oven to 150° C (300° F).

- Cook pasta in saucepan according to package directions. Drain and set aside.

- Sauté capsicum, onion and celery with butter in frypan.

- Add crabmeat, simmer for 8 to 10 minutes and stir occasionally.

- Add parsley, garlic and cream and mix well. Gradually stir in flour and mix well. Simmer for 30 minutes and stir occasionally.

- Add cheese and continue to stir until it melts and blends. Mix pasta with sauce.

- Pour all into sprayed 6-L (6-quart) baking dish. Bake for 15 to 20 minutes or until it is hot. Serves 8.

Alfredo Salmon and Fettuccini

3 cups (315 g) fettuccini (medium egg noodles) pasta
455 g (16 ounces) frozen broccoli florets, thawed
1 cup (250 ml) alfredo sauce
1 425-g (15-ounce) can salmon, drained, boned, flaked

- Cook pasta in large saucepan according to package directions and add broccoli last 5 minutes of cooking. (Discard some of broccoli stems.) Drain.

- Stir in alfredo sauce and salmon and cook on low heat, stirring occasionally, until mixture heats thoroughly. Spoon into serving bowl. Serves 6.

Cashew Tuna

1 280-g (10-ounce) can cream of mushroom soup
1 170-g (6-ounce) can tuna, drained
2 sticks celery, chopped
¼ cup (40 g) finely chopped onion
1 roasted red capsicum
85 g (3 ounces) cashew pieces
¾ cup (40 g) chow mein noodles

- Preheat oven to 175° C (350° F).

- Combine soup with ¼ cup (60 ml) water in large bowl and mix well. Stir in tuna, celery, onion, roasted red capsicum, cashews, ¼ cup (60 ml) chow mein noodles and a little black pepper.

- Pour into sprayed 2-L (2-quart) baking dish, sprinkle remaining noodles over top and bake for 30 minutes. Serves 4.

Tuna Casserole

230 g (8 ounces) elbow
   macaroni (tube) pasta
230 g (8 ounces) shredded processed
   cheese
2 170-g (6-ounce) cans tuna,
   drained
1 280-g (10-ounce) can cream
   of celery soup
1 cup (250 ml) milk

- Preheat oven to 175° C (350° F).

- Cook pasta in saucepan according
  to package directions. Drain well,
  add cheese and stir until cheese
  melts.

- Add tuna, celery soup and milk
  and continue stirring. Spoon into
  sprayed 18 x 28-cm (7 x 11-inch)
  baking dish. Cover and bake for
  35 minutes or until bubbly.
  Serves 6.

Tuna Linguine

230 g (8 ounces) linguine
   (thin egg noodles) pasta
280 g (10 ounces) frozen cut
   green beans
230 g (8 ounces) baby carrots,
   cut in half lengthwise
½ cup (125 g) pesto
⅓ cup (25 g) pouring cream
2 170-g (6-ounce) cans tuna,
   drained, flaked
½ cup (50 g) grated fresh
   parmesan cheese

- Cook pasta in large saucepan
  according to package directions.
  Drain and return to saucepan.
  Cover to keep warm.

- Cook green beans and carrots in
  microwave according to green bean
  package directions, drain.

- Add warm vegetables, pesto, cream
  and a little salt and pepper to pasta
  and toss to mix. Gently stir in tuna
  and spoon into serving bowl and
  sprinkle with parmesan cheese.
  Serves 8.

Tuna Pappardelle

230 g (8 ounces) pappardelle (wide
  egg noodles) pasta, cooked,
  drained
2 170-g (6-ounce) cans tuna, drained
1 280-g (10-ounce) can cream
  of chicken soup
¾ cup (175 ml) milk
¾ cup (95 g) chopped black olives

- Preheat oven to 150° C (300° F).

- Place half pasta in sprayed 2-L
  (2-quart) baking dish.

- Combine tuna, soup, milk and
  olives in saucepan. Heat just
  enough to mix well.

- Pour half soup mixture over pasta
  and repeat layers.

- Cover and bake for 20 minutes.
  Serves 6.

Tuna-Tomato Bowl

2 tablespoons (30 ml) olive oil
1 teaspoon minced garlic
¼ teaspoon cayenne pepper
2 teaspoons dried basil
1 425-g (15-ounce) can stewed
  tomatoes
1 340-g (12-ounce) can water-
  packed tuna, drained
¾ cup (95 g) pitted green olives,
  sliced
¼ cup (30 g) drained capers
1 cup (105 g) favourite pasta, cooked

- Heat olive oil in saucepan and add
  garlic, cayenne pepper and basil;
  cook on low heat for 2 minutes.
  Add tomatoes and bring to a boil,
  reduce heat and simmer for
  20 minutes.

- Combine tuna, olives, capers, pasta
  and a little salt in bowl. Stir in
  oil-tomato sauce and toss. Serve
  immediately. Serves 6.

Simple Pasta

These recipes have great appeal.
Use as side dishes or add
your favourite choice of meat
to turn into main dishes.

Simple Pasta Contents

Creamy Pasta

1 roasted red capsicum, chopped
½ litre (14 ounces) chicken stock
85 g (3 ounces) cream cheese
230 g (8 ounces) pasta, cooked

- Combine roasted red capsicum and stock in blender and mix well.

- Pour into saucepan and heat to boiling.

- Turn heat down and whisk in cream cheese. Serve over your favourite pasta. Serves 4.

Ranch Spaghetti

340 g (12 ounces) spaghetti pasta
¼ cup (60 g) butter, cut in 3 pieces
¾ cup (180 g) sour cream
¾ cup (175 ml) ranch dressing
½ cup (50 g) grated parmesan
   cheese

- Cook pasta in saucepan according to package directions, drain and return to saucepan. Stir in butter, sour cream and ranch dressing and toss. Spoon into serving bowl and sprinkle with grated parmesan cheese. Serves 8.

TIP: *You can make a main dish with this recipe just by adding 1 to 2 cups (140 to 420 g) cubed ham or turkey.*

Cheese-Spaghetti and Spinach

200 g (7 ounces) spaghetti pasta, broken
2 tablespoons (30 g) butter
230 g (8 ounces) sour cream
1 cup (115 g) shredded cheddar cheese
230 g (8 ounces) Colby cheese
340 g (12 ounces) frozen, chopped spinach, thawed, very well drained
1 onion, chopped, fried

- Cook pasta according to package directions, drain and stir in butter until it melts.

- Combine sour cream, cheddar cheese, half Colby cheese, spinach and onion in large bowl.

- Fold into pasta and spoon into sprayed slow cooker.

- Cover and cook on low for 2 to 4 hours.

- When ready to serve, sprinkle remaining cheese over top. Serves 4.

The word spaghetti is derived from the Italian word 'spago' meaning 'twine'. 'Spaghetto' means 'little twine' and 'spaghetti' is the plural form.

Ready Spaghetti and Veggies

455 g (16 ounces) frozen
    Italian style vegetables
2 tablespoons (15 g) cornflour
½ litre (14 ounces) carton chicken
    stock
1 teaspoon Italian seasoning
455 g (16 ounces) spaghetti pasta,
    cooked, drained
1 cup (115 g) shredded mozzarella
    cheese
¼ cup (30 g) grated parmesan
    cheese

- Microwave vegetables according to package directions, cover and set aside.

- Combine cornflour with ¼ cup (60 ml) stock in large saucepan and stir until cornflour dissolves. Add remaining stock and bring to a boil on medium-high heat, reduce heat, stirring constantly, until it thickens.

- Combine vegetables, sauce, Italian seasoning, pasta and mozzarella cheese in large bowl. Toss and mix thoroughly. Sprinkle parmesan cheese over top and serve immediately. Serves 6 to 8.

Vermicelli with Mushroom Sauce

1½ cups (110 g) sliced mushrooms
½ cup (80 g) chopped onion
1 stick celery, sliced
¼ cup (60 g) butter
1½ cups (10 ounces) beef stock
1 280-g (10-ounce) can cream
    of mushroom soup
¼ cup (60 ml) white wine
1 teaspoon (5 ml) Italian seasoning
230 g (8 ounces) vermicelli (thin
    spaghetti) pasta

- Sauté mushrooms, onions, celery and butter in frypan over medium heat. Stir in stock, mushroom soup, wine and Italian seasoning; mix well.

- Cook pasta in saucepan according to package directions, drain and return to saucepan. Spoon mushroom mixture over pasta and toss until mushroom sauce coats each ingredient. Serves 4 to 6.

Pasta Frittata

1 onion, chopped
1 green capsicum, seeded, chopped
1 red capsicum, seeded, chopped
2 tablespoons (30 g) butter
200 g (7 ounces) vermicelli
    (thin spaghetti) pasta,
    slightly broken, cooked
230 g (8 ounces) shredded
    mozzarella cheese
5 eggs
1 cup (250 ml) milk
⅓ cup (35 g) shredded parmesan
    cheese
1 tablespoon (15 ml) dried basil
1 teaspoon oregano

- Preheat oven to 190° C (375° F).

- Sauté onion and capsicums with butter in frypan over medium heat for about 5 minutes, but do not brown.

- Combine onion-capsicum mixture and pasta in large bowl and toss. Add mozzarella cheese and toss.

- In separate bowl, beat eggs, milk, parmesan cheese, basil, oregano, ½ teaspoon each of salt and pepper. Add pasta mixture and pour into sprayed 23 x 33-cm (9 x 13-inch) baking dish.

- Cover and bake for about 15 to 20 minutes. Uncover and make sure eggs are set. If not, bake for additional 2 to 3 minutes. Serves 8.

TIP: *This can be put together, refrigerated and baked later. Let it get to room temperature before placing in oven. Cut into squares to serve. It is a great dish for lunch or late night dinner.*

Favourite Pasta

115 g (4 ounces) spinach linguine
   (thin egg noodles) pasta
1 cup (75 g) pouring cream
1 cup (250 ml) chicken stock
½ cup (50 g) freshly grated
   parmesan cheese
½ cup (50 g) frozen English peas

- Cook pasta in saucepan according to package directions, drain and keep warm. Combine cream and chicken stock in saucepan and bring to a boil.

- Reduce heat and simmer mixture for 25 minutes or until it thickens and reduces to 1 cup (250 ml). Remove from heat, add cheese and peas and stir until cheese melts.

- Toss with pasta and serve immediately. Serves 4.

Love This Linguine

2 tablespoons (30 ml) olive oil
2 teaspoons minced garlic
2 red capsicums, seeded,
   chopped
½ teaspoon cayenne pepper
1 cup (150 g) roasted red capsicum,
   drained, diced
340 g (12 ounces) linguine (thin egg
   noodles) pasta, cooked,
   drained
¾ cup (75 g) grated parmesan
   cheese, divided

- Heat oil in heavy frypan over medium-high and sauté garlic, capsicums, cayenne pepper and a little salt for about 5 minutes. Remove from heat and add roasted red capsicum, linguine and ½ cup (50 g) parmesan cheese and mix well.

- Transfer to serving bowl and sprinkle remaining parmesan cheese over top. Serves 4.

Artichoke Fettuccini

340 g (12 ounces) fettuccini (medium
    egg noodles) pasta
1 400-g (14-ounce) can water-
    packed artichoke hearts,
    drained, chopped
280 g (10 ounces) frozen
    green peas, thawed
1 455-g (16-ounce) jar alfredo
    sauce
2 heaped tablespoons (30 g)
    crumbled blue cheese

- Cook pasta in saucepan according
  to package directions. Drain and
  place in serving bowl to keep
  warm.

- Heat artichoke hearts, peas and
  alfredo sauce in large saucepan.
  Stir well, spoon into bowl with
  pasta and toss. Sprinkle
  with blue cheese and serve hot.
  Serves 10.

Cheesy Pasta Casserole

230 g (8 ounces) fettuccini (medium
    egg noodles) pasta
455 g (16 ounces) frozen
    broccoli florets, thawed
1 red capsicum, seeded, chopped
230 g (8 ounces) shredded processed
    cheese
1 cup (250 ml) milk
¾ cup (45 g) coarsely crushed
    bite-size cheese biscuits

- Preheat oven to 175° C (350° F).

- Cook pasta in large saucepan
  according to package directions.
  Add broccoli and capsicum for last
  2 minutes of cooking time. Drain in
  colander.

- In same saucepan, combine cheese
  and milk over low heat and stir
  until cheese melts. Stir in pasta-
  broccoli mixture and spoon into
  sprayed 3-L (3-quart) baking dish.

- Sprinkle with crushed biscuits and
  bake for 25 to 30 minutes or until
  top is golden brown. Serves 10.

Buttered Pasta Casserole

680 g (24 ounces) fettuccini (medium egg noodles) pasta
1¼ cups (285 g) butter
¼ cup (25 g) grated parmesan cheese
½ cup (50 g) grated romano cheese
455 g (16 ounces) frozen green peas, thawed
1 cup (60 g) fresh breadcrumbs
½ teaspoon cayenne pepper

- Preheat oven at 190° C (375° F).

- Cook pasta in large saucepan according to package directions and drain; return to saucepan.

- In separate saucepan, melt 1 cup (230 g) butter and stir into pasta. Add parmesan and romano cheese, peas and a little salt. Stir until mixture combines well and spoon into sprayed 4-L (4-quart) baking dish.

- Melt remaining butter and toss with breadcrumbs and cayenne pepper. Sprinkle over pasta and bake for 15 minutes or until edges are bubbly. Serves 10 to 12.

Noodles are mentioned in the Jerusalem Talmud, a Jewish text from around 200 A.D. Wheat has been grown in the Middle East for 8,000 to 10,000 years. It is thought that some ancient form of pasta would have been made because of the evidence of the use of wheat flour.

Dreamy Baked Fettuccini

455 g (16 ounces) fettuccini (medium
   egg noodles) pasta
½ cup (115 g) butter, cut
   into chunks
1 cup (250 ml) unthickened
   cream
3 large eggs, beaten
1½ cups (150 g) grated parmesan
   cheese
⅓ cup (40 g) seasoned
   breadcrumbs

- Preheat oven to 175° C (350° F).

- Cook pasta in saucepan according
  to package directions, drain and
  return to saucepan. Add butter and
  stir until butter melts.

- Stir in cream, eggs and 1 cup
  (100 g) parmesan cheese and spoon
  into sprayed 3-quart (3-L) baking
  dish.

- Combine remaining cheese and
  breadcrumbs in bowl and sprinkle
  over pasta. Bake for 25 minutes.
  Serves 8.

Favourite Fettuccini

455 g (16 ounces) fettuccini (medium
   egg noodles) pasta
2 tablespoons (30 g) butter
¾ cup (75 g) grated fresh
   parmesan cheese
1¼ cups (95 g) pouring cream

- Cook pasta in saucepan according
  to package directions.

- Melt butter in large saucepan over
  medium heat and stir in parmesan
  cheese, cream and a little
  black pepper.

- Cook for 1 minute and stir
  constantly. Reduce heat, pour
  in pasta and toss gently to
  coat. Serves 6.

Faithful Fettuccini Fiesta

3 tablespoons (45 ml) olive oil
1 yellow capsicum, seeded, chopped
1 onion, chopped
2 teaspoons minced garlic
2 slices, fried, diced bacon
2 roasted red capsicums, sliced
280 g (10 ounces) frozen baby green
    peas, thawed
⅓ cup (75 ml) chicken stock
230 g (8 ounces) fettuccini (medium
    egg noodles) pasta,
    cooked, drained
½ cup (60 g) shredded mozzarella
    cheese

- Heat oil in large frypan on medium-high and cook yellow capsicum, onion and garlic for about 4 minutes.

- Stir in bacon, roasted red capsicums, peas and stock; reduce heat to low and simmer for 10 minutes.

- Transfer to large bowl and toss with cooked pasta, cheese and a little salt and pepper. (You might want to garnish with more mozzarella cheese.) Serves 4 to 6.

Not Your Ordinary Pasta

455 g (16 ounces) fettuccini (medium
   egg noodles) pasta
½ cup (115 g) butter, melted
455 g (16 ounces) cottage cheese,
   drained
230 g (8 ounces) cream cheese,
   softened
455 g (16 ounces) sour cream
1 teaspoon vanilla
1 cup (200 g) sugar
¾ cup (165 g) packed brown sugar
6 large eggs, beaten
2 cups (210 g) cheese biscuit crumbs
½ cup (115 g) butter, melted
⅔ cup (135 g) sugar
½ cup (55 g) chopped pecans

- Preheat oven to 190° C (375° F).

- Cook pasta in large saucepan according to package directions and drain. Place in large bowl and stir in ½ cup (115 g) melted butter. Cover and keep warm.

- Beat cottage cheese and cream cheese in mixing bowl until smooth. Stir in sour cream, vanilla, sugar, brown sugar and eggs; mix until they blend well.

- Fold mixture into buttered pasta, mix well and spoon into sprayed 23 x 33-cm (9 x 13-inch) baking pan.

- Combine biscuit crumbs, butter, sugar and pecans in bowl, mix well and sprinkle evenly over top of pasta mixture. Bake for 15 minutes.

- Reduce heat to 160° C (325° F) and bake for additional 40 minutes. Cool to room temperature before cutting into squares to serve. Serves 18.

Speedy Zucchini and Fettuccini

255 g (9 ounces) refrigerated fresh
    fettuccini (medium
    egg noodles) pasta
⅓ cup (75 ml) extra-virgin olive oil
1 tablespoon (15 ml) minced garlic
4 small zucchini, grated
1 tablespoon (15 ml) lemon juice
½ cup (65 g) pine nuts, toasted
⅓ cup (30 g) grated parmesan
    cheese

- Cook pasta in saucepan according to package directions, drain and place in serving bowl.

- Heat large frypan over high heat and add 2 tablespoons (30 ml) oil, garlic and zucchini. Sauté for 1 minute.

- Add zucchini mixture to pasta with lemon juice, pine nuts and a little salt and pepper.

- Stir in remaining olive oil and toss to combine. Sprinkle parmesan cheese over top of dish to serve. Serves 8 to 10.

St. Pat's Pasta

340 g (12 ounces) fettuccini (medium
    egg noodles) pasta
1 cup (310 g) unthickened cream
280 g (10 ounces) frozen chopped
    spinach, thawed
6 tablespoons (90 g) butter, melted
2 teaspoons seasoned salt
1½ cups (175 g) shredded cheddar
    cheese

- Cook pasta in saucepan according to package directions and drain.

- Place in 5 to 6-L (5 to 6-quart) slow cooker. Add cream, spinach, butter and seasoned salt and stir until they blend well.

- Cover and cook on low for 2 to 3 hours.

- When ready to serve, fold in cheese. Serves 4.

Wonderful Alfredo Fettuccini

910 g (32 ounces) fettuccini (medium
   egg noodles) pasta
¼ cup (60 g) butter
1½ cups (150 g) grated fresh
   parmesan cheese
2½ cups (190 g) pouring cream

- Cook pasta in saucepan according
  to package directions.

- Melt butter in large saucepan over
  medium heat and stir in parmesan
  cheese, cream and a little salt. Cook
  for 2 minutes and stir constantly.
  Reduce heat, stir into pasta and toss
  gently to coat pasta.
  Serves 10 to 12.

Creamy Seasoned Pappardelle

230 g (8 ounces) pappardelle (wide
   egg noodles) pasta
30 g (1 ounce) French
   onion soup mix
½ cup (40 g) pouring cream
¼ cup (60 g) butter
¼ cup (30 g) grated parmesan
   cheese

- Cook pasta in saucepan according
  to package directions and drain.

- Add remaining ingredients and toss
  lightly to blend thoroughly.

- Serve hot. Serves 6.

TIP: *Cut butter in chunks so it will*
       melt more easily.

Creamy Macaroni and Cheese

Yes, this is more trouble than opening a box, but it is well worth the time to make this macaroni and cheese.

340 g (12 ounces) macaroni (tube) pasta
6 tablespoons (90 g) butter
¼ cup (30 g) flour
2 cups (500 ml) milk
1 455-g (1-pound) package cubed processed cheese

- Preheat oven to 175° C (350° F).

- Cook pasta in saucepan according to package directions and drain.

- Melt butter in saucepan and stir in flour, ½ teaspoon each of salt and pepper until they blend well.

- Slowly add milk, stirring constantly, and heat until it begins to thicken. Add cheese and stir until cheese melts.

- Pour cheese sauce over pasta and mix well.

- Pour into sprayed 2.5-L (2½-quart) baking dish. Cover and bake for 30 minutes or until bubbly. Serves 8.

Tube pastas, like macaroni and penne, and shapes like shells work very well for casseroles and salads. Fresh pasta and egg noodle pasta are suitable for salads.

Double Pleasure Pasta

¼ cup (60 ml) olive oil
1 onion, chopped
3 teaspoons minced garlic
1½ tablespoons (22 ml) dried
    oregano
¼–½ teaspoon crushed chilli
2 425-g (15-ounce) can diced
    tomatoes
1 cup (130 g) sliced green olives
1 cup (130 g) sliced black olives
340 g (12 ounces) wholemeal elbow
    macaroni (tube) pasta
230 g (8 ounces) shredded
    mozzarella cheese

- With oil in soup pot over medium-high heat, sauté onion, garlic and oregano for 5 minutes. Stir in chilli, tomatoes, green and black olives and bring to a boil. Reduce heat to medium, stir often and simmer for about 6 minutes or until sauce begins to thicken.

- Cook pasta in saucepan according to package directions, drain and stir in ½ teaspoon salt.

- Add pasta and 1½ cups (170 g) cheese to onion-tomato mixture and toss. Transfer to serving bowl and sprinkle with remaining cheese. Serves 8.

Wholemeal pasta has more nutrition than plain pasta. The wholemeal flour makes it darker which adds interesting colour.

Good Stuff Macaroni

455 g (16 ounces) macaroni (tube) pasta
2 eggs, well beaten
½ cup (115 g) butter
1 cup (160 g) finely chopped onion
1 cup (150 g) finely chopped green capsicum
230 g (8 ounces) pouring cream
230 g (8 ounces) shredded sharp cheddar cheese
½ cup (60 g) shredded Swiss cheese
½ cup (60 g) shredded mozzarella cheese

- Preheat oven to 175° C (350° F).

- Cook pasta in saucepan according to package directions. Rinse in cold water, drain and return to saucepan. Add beaten eggs, mix well and spoon into sprayed 23 x 33-cm (9 x 13-inch) baking dish.

- Melt butter in large saucepan over medium heat and sauté onion and capsicum just until they wilt. Stir in cream and a little salt and pepper. Reduce heat to low and gradually add half cheddar cheese, Swiss cheese and finally mozzarella. Stir constantly as you add cheeses so they do no stick to saucepan and burn.

- Pour cheese sauce evenly over pasta and stir just a little to incorporate sauce into pasta.

- Sprinkle remaining cheddar cheese over top and bake for 40 to 45 minutes or until cheese on top melts and starts to brown. Serves 8.

Cheesy Mac Florentine

455 g (16 ounces) elbow macaroni
  (tube) pasta
340 g (12 ounces) frozen spinach
  quiche, crust removed
¼ cup (60 ml) milk
230 g (8 ounces) shredded
  mozzarella cheese
¼ cup (25 g) grated parmesan
  cheese
½ cup (60 g) seasoned breadcrumbs

- Preheat oven to 175° C (350° F).

- Bring large pot of salted water to a
  boil. Add pasta, cook until al dente
  and drain.

- Cut spinach quiche into 2.5-cm
  (1-inch) pieces stir into pasta. Add
  milk and both cheeses; mix well.

- Spoon into sprayed 23 x 33-cm
  (9 x 13-inch) baking dish and
  sprinkle breadcrumbs over top.
  Bake for 15 minutes. Serves 6.

Macaroni and Cheese

1 cup (105 g) macaroni (tube) pasta
1½ cups (340 g) cottage cheese
1½ cups (175 g) shredded cheddar
  cheese
4 tablespoons (50 g) grated
  parmesan cheese

- Preheat oven to 175° C (350° F).

- Cook pasta in saucepan according
  to package directions and drain.
  Combine cottage cheese and both
  cheeses. Combine pasta with
  cheese mixture.

- Spoon into sprayed 2-L (2-quart)
  baking dish.

- Cover and bake for 35 minutes.
  Serves 4.

Macaroni and Cheese Deluxe

230 g (8 ounces) macaroni (tube)
  pasta
3 tablespoons (45 g) butter, melted
1 425-g (15-ounce) can stewed
  tomatoes
230 g (8 ounces) shredded cheddar
  cheese
1 cup (55 g) crushed potato chips,
  optional

- Preheat oven to 175° C (350° F).

- Cook pasta in saucepan according
  to package directions, drain and
  place in bowl. While pasta is still
  hot, stir in butter, tomatoes, cheese
  and a little salt and pepper and mix
  well.

- Pour into sprayed 2-L (2-quart)
  baking dish, cover and bake for
  25 minutes. Uncover and sprinkle
  with crushed potato chips. Bake
  for additional 10 minutes or until
  potato chips are light brown.
  Serves 8.

Macaroni and Cheese Reward

2 cups (210 g) macaroni (tube)
  pasta
2 cups (500 ml) milk
¼ cup (30 g) flour
455 g (16 ounces) shredded sharp
  cheddar cheese
¼ cup (60 g) melted butter
1 cup (60 g) soft breadcrumbs

- Preheat oven to 175° C (350° F).

- Cook pasta in saucepan according
  to package directions, drain and
  set aside. Combine milk, flour and
  ample amount of seasoned salt in
  jar with lid. Shake to mix well.

- Combine pasta, flour-milk mixture
  and cheese in large bowl and mix
  well. Pour into sprayed
  23 x 33-cm (9 x 13-inch) baking
  dish. Stir melted butter over
  breadcrumbs in bowl and toss.
  Sprinkle breadcrumbs over top.

- Cover and bake for 35 minutes;
  remove cover and return to oven
  for 10 minutes. Serves 6.

Macaroni, Cheese and Tomatoes

2 cups (210 g) elbow macaroni
    (tube) pasta
1 400-g (14-ounce) can stewed
    tomatoes with liquid
230 g (8 ounces) shredded cheddar
    cheese
2 tablespoons (25 g) sugar
170 g (6 ounces) cheese slices

- Preheat oven to 175° C (350° F).

- Cook pasta in saucepan according
  to package directions and drain.
  Combine pasta, tomatoes, shredded
  cheese, sugar, ¼ cup (60 ml) water
  and a little salt in large mixing
  bowl and mix well.

- Pour into 23 x 33-cm (9 x 13-inch)
  baking dish and place cheese
  slices on top.

- Bake for 30 minutes or until
  bubbly. Serves 6.

Magic Macaroni and Veggies

230 g (8 ounces) macaroni (tube)
    pasta
3 eggs, beaten
1¼ cups (310 g) milk
1 cup (60 g) soft breadcrumbs
1½ teaspoons seasoned salt
1 425-g (15-ounce) can diced
    tomatoes
230 g (8 ounces) shredded cheddar
    cheese
1 onion, chopped
1 red capsicum, chopped
280 g (10 ounces) frozen chopped
    carrots and green peas, thawed

- Preheat oven to 175° C (350° F).

- Cook pasta in saucepan according
  to package directions, drain and
  place in large bowl.

- Stir in eggs, milk, breadcrumbs,
  seasoned salt, tomatoes, cheese,
  onions and capsicum, and
  carrot and peas. Bake for
  1 hour 5 minutes. Serves 8.

Minute Mac and Cheese

340 g (12 ounces) elbow macaroni (tube) pasta
230 g (8 ounces) shredded cheddar cheese
¾ cup (85 g) shredded mozzarella cheese
1¼ cups (310 ml) milk
1 teaspoon mustard

- Preheat oven to 160° C (325° F).

- Cook pasta in saucepan according to package directions and drain. Stir in cheddar cheese, mozzarella cheese, milk and mustard and mix until they blend well.

- Transfer to sprayed 3-L (3-quart) baking dish, cover and bake for 10 minutes or just until thoroughly hot. Serves 8.

Pasta with Basil

2½ cups (260 g) macaroni (tube) pasta
1 small onion, chopped
2 tablespoons (30 ml) olive oil
2½ tablespoons (35 ml) dried basil
1 cup (115 g) shredded mozzarella cheese

- Cook pasta in saucepan according to package directions. Sauté onion in oil in frypan.

- Stir in basil, 1 teaspoon salt (5 ml) and ¼ teaspoon pepper. Cook and stir for 1 minute. Drain pasta leaving about ½ cup (125 ml) so pasta won't be too dry and add to basil mixture.

- Remove from heat and stir in cheese just until it begins to melt. Serve immediately. Serves 6.

So-Easy Macaroni Bake

**230 g (8 ounces) elbow
    macaroni (tube) pasta
2 tablespoons (30 ml) olive oil
4 large eggs
2¼ cups (560 ml) milk
1 cup (135 g) crumbled feta cheese
1 cup (225 g) cottage cheese
1 roasted red capsicum, chopped**

- Preheat oven to 190° C (375° F).

- Cook pasta in saucepan according to package directions, drain and stir in olive oil. Transfer to sprayed 23 x 33-cm (9 x 13-inch) baking dish.

- Beat eggs in medium bowl with fork and stir in milk, feta cheese, cottage cheese, roasted red capsicum and ½ teaspoon salt.

- Pour cheese mixture over pasta in baking dish, cover and bake for 40 minutes. Uncover dish and return to oven for 10 minutes.

- Let pasta stand for 10 minutes before serving. Serves 8.

Special Macaroni and Cheese

**230 g (8 ounces) gnocchi pasta
1 425-g (15-ounce) can stewed
    tomatoes
230 g (8 ounces) cubed
    cheddar cheese
3 tablespoons (45 g) butter, melted**

- Preheat oven to 175° C (350° F).

- Cook pasta in saucepan according to package directions and drain.

- Combine pasta, tomatoes, cheese and butter in large bowl.

- Pour into sprayed 2-L (2-quart) baking dish.

- Cover and bake for 35 minutes. Serves 6.

Southern Macaroni and Cheese

455 g (16 ounces) macaroni (tube) pasta
2 tablespoons (30 g) butter
3 eggs, beaten
455 g (16 ounces) unthickened cream
340 g (12 ounces) cheddar cheese
⅛ teaspoon cayenne pepper

- Preheat oven to 175° C (350° F).

- Combine pasta and 2 teaspoons salt in large saucepan and cook for 6 minutes. (Pasta should not cook completely.)

- Drain pasta and stir in butter to keep it from sticking. Transfer to sprayed 2.5-L (2½-quart) baking dish.

- Combine eggs, cream, three-fourths cheese and cayenne pepper in bowl and mix well. Pour mixture over pasta and sprinkle remaining cheese over top.

- Cover and bake for 35 minutes. Uncover and grill just enough to lightly brown top. Serves 8.

Creamy King Cavatappi

455 g (16 ounces) cavatappi
    (corkscrew) pasta
2 tablespoons (30 ml) olive oil
3 tablespoons (40 g) butter
1 onion, finely chopped
2 sticks celery, thinly sliced
230 g (8 ounces) pouring cream
¼ cup (30 g) sliced black olives
340 g (12 ounces) shredded
    processed cheese
2 teaspoons dried parsley

- Preheat oven to 175° C (350° F).

- Cook pasta in saucepan according to package directions, rinse in cold water and drain in colander. Drizzle in olive oil and stir. Make sure each piece of pasta has oil on it. Transfer to sprayed 23 x 33-cm (9 x 13-inch) baking dish.

- Melt butter in large frypan and sauté onion and celery until they are soft. Turn heat to high and add cream, stirring constantly. Cook until mixture begins to thicken. (Mixture needs to be reduced to half original volume.)

- Slowly add olives, cheese, parsley and a little salt and pepper; stir until sauce blends well.

- Pour cheese sauce evenly over pasta in baking dish. With large spoon work cheese sauce until sauce absorbs into pasta.

- Bake for about 15 minutes or until casserole is piping hot. Serves 8 to 10.

Wild About Macaroni

230 g (8 ounces) elbow macaroni
  (tube) pasta
½ cup (110 g) mayonnaise
½ cup (75 g) finely chopped green
  capsicum
1 small onion, finely chopped
2 roasted red capsicums, chopped
1 280-g (10-ounce) can cream
  of celery soup
2 tablespoons (30 g) butter, melted
1 cup (115 g) shredded cheddar
  cheese
1 cup (250 ml) milk

- Preheat oven to 190° C (375° F).

- Cook pasta in saucepan according
  to package directions, drain and
  place in large bowl.

- Add mayonnaise, capsicum, onion,
  roasted red capsicum, celery soup,
  butter, half cheese and a little
  salt and pepper.

- Spoon mixture into sprayed
  2-L (2-quart) baking dish. Top
  with remaining cheese and add
  milk. Bake for 20 to 25 minutes.
  Serves 8.

Pasta Alarm!

230 g (8 ounces) tri-colour cavatappi
  (corkscrew) pasta
2 tablespoons (30 ml) olive oil
1 green capsicum, seeded,
  chopped
1 onion, chopped
2 teaspoons minced garlic
1 teaspoon chilli powder
1 teaspoon ground cumin
½ teaspoon crushed chilli flakes
1 230-g (8-ounce) can tomato soup
1 425-g (15-ounce) can lentils,
  rinsed, drained
1 cup (115 g) shredded cheddar
  cheese

- Cook pasta in saucepan according
  to package directions and drain.
  Heat oil in large frypan on medium
  and cook capsicum, onion, garlic,
  chilli powder, cumin and chilli
  flakes for about 5 minutes.

- Stir in tomato soup, lentils and a
  little salt. Bring to a boil, reduce
  heat and simmer for 5 minutes or
  until thoroughly hot. Gently stir in
  pasta and mix well. Sprinkle with
  cheese. Serves 6 to 8.

Penne and Vegetables

230 g (8 ounces) penne (tube) pasta
2 tablespoons (30 ml) olive oil
½ cup (80 g) chopped onion
½ cup (75 g) chopped green
    capsicum
1 carrot, peeled, chopped
1 teaspoon minced garlic
1 425-g (15-ounce) can cannellini
    beans, drained
1 425-g (15-ounce) can stewed
    tomatoes
½ cup (50 g) grated parmesan
    cheese

- Cook pasta according to package directions and drain. Place in serving bowl, cover and keep warm.

- Heat oil in large saucepan over medium-high heat and cook onion, capsicum, carrot and garlic for 6 minutes or until vegetables are tender but crisp, stirring frequently.

- Stir in beans and tomatoes; bring to a boil. Reduce heat to medium-low and simmer for 6 minutes or until mixture is thoroughly hot. Serve over penne pasta and sprinkle with parmesan cheese. Serves 8.

Tomatoes met pasta in the 17th century when tomatoes were first imported from the Americas. Eight species of tomato still grow in the wild in Peru.

Ready to Please Pasta

230 g (8 ounces) penne (tube) pasta
1 onion, chopped
1 cup (100 g) chopped celery
2 teaspoons minced garlic
1 tablespoon (15 ml) olive oil
**1 425-g (15-ounce) can Italian
      stewed tomatoes**
**1 425-g (15-ounce) can cannellini
      beans, rinsed, drained**
1½ cups (10 ounces) chicken stock
**¾ cup (85 g) shredded mozzarella
      cheese**
**280 g (10 ounces) frozen chopped
      spinach, thawed, drained**

- Preheat oven to 190° C (375° F).

- Cook pasta in large saucepan according to package directions, drain and return pasta to saucepan.

- Sauté onion, celery and garlic with oil in frypan on medium-high heat until tender. Stir in tomatoes, beans, stock, ¼ cup (30 g) cheese and ½ teaspoon pepper. Bring to a boil and stir in spinach.

- Spoon onion-bean mixture into saucepan with pasta and toss until they mix well.

- Transfer to sprayed 3-L (3-quart) baking dish and sprinkle remaining cheese on top. Bake for 15 minutes or until centre is hot and top is golden. Serves 8.

Zucchini and Creamy Penne

6–8 medium zucchini, sliced
2 tablespoons (30 ml) olive oil
2 455-g (16-ounce) penne (tube)
    pasta
460 g (16 ounces) pouring cream
340 g (12 ounces) crumbled goat
    cheese

- Cook zucchini in saucepan with a little salted water, drain and add olive oil.

- In separate saucepan, cook pasta according to package directions. Drain and add remaining olive oil.

- While zucchini and pasta are still hot, combine ingredients in bowl, stir in cream and goat cheese and toss. Serve hot. Serves 8.

Creamy Tomato Pasta

230 g (8 ounces) penne (tube) pasta
1 740-g (26-ounce) jar pasta sauce
½ cup (60 g) shredded mozzarella
    cheese
½ cup (155 g) unthickened cream
½ cup (50 g) grated parmesan
    cheese

- Cook penne pasta in saucepan according to package directions, drain and keep warm.

- Combine pasta sauce, mozzarella cheese and cream in saucepan and cook over medium heat, stirring often, until mixture is thoroughly hot and slightly thick. Pour over penne and toss to mix.

- Transfer to serving bowl and sprinkle parmesan cheese over mixture. Serves 8.

A Different Spaghetti Sauce

2 tablespoons (30 ml) olive oil
2 teaspoons minced garlic
1 stick celery, finely sliced
1 red capsicum, seeded,
    finely chopped
2 425-g (15-ounce) cans Italian
    stewed tomatoes
8 anchovies, chopped
12 black olives, sliced
1 teaspoon capers
1 teaspoon dried basil
¼ teaspoon chilli flakes
230 g (8 ounces) ziti (thin tubes)
    pasta
2 tablespoons (30 g) butter

- Heat oil in large frypan and sauté garlic, celery and capsicum for about 5 minutes.

- Press tomatoes through sieve or food mill and add to frypan along with anchovies. Bring to a boil, reduce heat to medium and cook for 10 minutes. Stir in olives, capers, basil, chilli and a little salt and simmer for an additional 15 minutes.

- Cook pasta in saucepan according to package directions, drain and return pasta to saucepan. Stir in butter until butter melts. Pour onto heated serving bowl and pour sauce over pasta. Serve immediately. Serves 6 to 8.

What does 'al dente' mean? Literally, it means 'to the tooth'. Pasta cooked al dente is completely cooked, but it is still a little firm when bitten into. Many people prefer their pasta al dente. Always begin testing pasta before the cooking time is up to be sure it is not overcooked and mushy.

A Summertime Deal

**340 g (12 ounces) ziti
   (thin tubes) pasta**
¼ cup (60 ml) olive oil
1 bunch spring onions, chopped
1 teaspoon minced garlic
**1 cup (75 g) halved cherry
   tomatoes**
**280 g (10 ounces) frozen
   green peas, thawed, drained**
**230 g (8 ounces) cubed cheddar
   cheese**
**115 g (4 ounces) fresh basil, torn
   in thirds**
**1 115-g (4-ounce) can chopped
   black olives, drained**
½ cup (125 ml) Italian salad dressing
**½ cup (50 g) grated parmesan
   cheese**

- Cook pasta in saucepan according to package directions, drain and set aside.

- Heat oil in large frypan and sauté spring onions, garlic, tomatoes and a little salt and pepper for about 3 minutes.

- Stir in pasta, green peas, cheese, basil, olives and salad dressing.

- Toss well and sprinkle parmesan cheese over top. Serve immediately. Serves 6.

Florentine Manicotti

455 g (16 ounces) manicotti (large
    tubes) pasta
340 g (12 ounces) frozen spinach
    quiche, crust removed
2 tablespoons (30 ml) finely
    chopped red capsicum
425 g (15 ounces) ricotta cheese
1 cup (120 g) breadcrumbs
1 teaspoon Italian seasoning
1 425-g (15-ounce) can Italian
    stewed tomatoes

- Preheat oven to 160° C (325° F).

- Cook pasta in saucepan according
  to package directions. Drain and
  place each tube on baking paper.
  Cook spinach quiche in microwave
  according to package directions.

- Combine cooked spinach quiche,
  capsicum, ricotta cheese, seasoning
  and breadcrumbs in large bowl.
  Carefully stuff mixture into pasta
  tubes and place in sprayed baking
  pan.

- Cover pasta with stewed tomatoes
  and bake for 15 minutes or until
  thoroughly hot. Serves 8.

Red Capsicum and Rotini

230 g (8 ounces) refrigerated
    wholemeal rotini (spiral) pasta
2 tablespoons (30 ml) olive oil
1 onion, finely chopped
1 stick celery, finely chopped
2 teaspoons minced garlic
1½ cups (200 g) roasted red
    capsicums, drained
½ cup (125 ml) evaporated milk
⅛ teaspoon cayenne pepper

- Cook pasta in saucepan according
  to package directions, drain and
  return pasta to saucepan. Toss with
  1 tablespoon (15 ml) oil, cover and
  keep warm.

- Heat remaining oil in frypan, cook
  and stir onion, celery and garlic on
  medium heat for about 3 minutes.

- Place onion-celery mixture, roasted
  red capsicums, evaporated milk and
  cayenne pepper in food processor
  and puree until smooth. Spoon
  sauce over pasta and stir to coat
  well. Serve immediately. Serves 4.

Merry Manicotti

425 g (15 ounces) ricotta cheese
2 eggs
280 g (10 ounces) frozen
**   chopped spinach,**
**   thawed, drained**
1½ cups (170 g) shredded
**   mozzarella cheese**
1 tablespoon (15 ml) sugar
12 manicotti (large tubes) pasta
1 795-g (28-ounce) jar spaghetti
**   sauce**
⅓ cup (35 g) grated parmesan
**   cheese**

- Beat ricotta cheese and eggs in bowl. Stir in spinach, mozzarella cheese, sugar and ½ teaspoon (2 ml) each of salt and pepper; mix well. Stuff cheese-spinach mixture into uncooked pasta tubes.

- Pour ½ cup (125 ml) spaghetti sauce and ¼ cup (60 ml) water in sprayed 23 x 33-cm (9 x 13-inch) baking pan. Arrange stuffed pasta tubes in single layer over sauce and pour remaining sauce over pasta tubes. Cover and refrigerate for 8 hours.

- When ready to bake, preheat oven to 190° C (375° F).

- Let pasta sit at room temperature for 10 to 15 minutes. Cover and bake for 45 minutes. Uncover, sprinkle parmesan cheese over top of pasta and bake for additional 10 minutes. Serves 8.

Spinach-Cheese Lumache

This does take a little extra time to fill the shells, but it is really a special dish and well worth the time it takes!

1 onion, minced
2 teaspoons minced garlic
Olive oil
425 g (15 ounces) ricotta cheese
85 g (3 ounces) cream cheese, softened
230 g (8 ounces) shredded mozzarella cheese
85 g (3 ounces) grated parmesan cheese
2 teaspoons Italian seasoning
280 g (10 ounces) frozen chopped spinach, thawed, drained
9 lumache (wide shells) pasta, cooked
1 740-g (26-ounce) jar spaghetti sauce

- Preheat oven to 175° C (350° F).

- Sauté onion and garlic in a little oil in frypan and set aside.

- Combine ricotta, cream cheese, half mozzarella, half parmesan cheese, Italian seasoning, ½ teaspoon each of salt and pepper in mixing bowl and beat until blended well.

- Squeeze spinach between paper towels to completely remove excess moisture.

- Add spinach and onion to cheese mixture and mix well.

- Spoon this mixture into pasta shells 1 teaspoon at a time. (Be careful not to tear shells.)

- Pour half of spaghetti sauce in sprayed 23 x 33-cm (9 x 13-inch) baking dish. Arrange pasta over sauce and top with remaining sauce.

- Cover and bake for 30 minutes. Remove from oven, uncover and sprinkle remaining cheeses over top. Return to oven just until cheese melts. Serves 9.

Tonight Is Fresh and Fast

2 red onions
2 sticks celery
2 tablespoons (30 ml) olive oil
1 red capsicum, seeded, sliced
1 green capsicum, seeded, sliced
230 g (8 ounces) fresh mushrooms,
    sliced
455 g (16 ounces) rigatoni (large
    tubes) pasta
1 teaspoon dried basil
1½ cups (200 g) cubed provolone
    cheese

- Cut onions crosswise and slice. Cut celery in 2.5-cm (1-inch) slices. Cook onions and celery with oil in large, heavy frypan over high heat for about 8 minutes and stir often.

- Reduce heat to medium-high, add capsicums and mushrooms and sauté for about 8 minutes or until they are soft.

- Cook pasta in saucepan according to package directions and stir occasionally. Drain, but reserve ½ cup (125 ml) cooking liquid.

- Add reserved pasta liquid to onion-mushroom mixture, basil and ½ teaspoon salt; stir over medium-high heat. Add 1 cup (130 g) cheese and stir until cheese melts. Transfer pasta to serving bowl, pour sauce over pasta and toss. Sprinkle with remaining cheese. Serves 6.

Stuffed Jumbo Shells

12 jumbo pasta shells
½ litre (14 ounces) chicken
 (or vegetable) stock
1 potato, peeled, finely chopped
1 carrot, peeled, finely chopped
1 zucchini, cut into 1.2-cm (½-inch)
 pieces
½ cup (160 g) finely chopped onion
1 teaspoon dried basil leaves
⅓ cup (35 g) grated parmesan
 cheese
3 tablespoons (20 g) seasoned
 breadcrumbs

- Preheat oven to 190° C (375° F).

- Cook pasta shells according to package directions, drain and place on sheet of baking paper.

- Heat stock to boiling in large saucepan and stir in potato and carrot and cook for about 6 minutes. Stir in zucchini and onion and cook for additional 3 minutes. Drain vegetables and set aside broth.

- Combine vegetables, basil, 3 tablespoons (30 g) cheese and 1 tablespoon (15 ml) breadcrumbs. Carefully fill cooked pasta shells with mixture and place sides up in sprayed 20-cm (8-inch) square baking dish. Pour set-aside stock into dish with pasta.

- Mix remaining cheese and breadcrumbs and sprinkle over pasta. Bake for 12 minutes or until breadcrumbs are golden brown. When serving, spoon broth from dish over pasta. Serves 4 to 6.

Fusilli with Garden Sauce

2 onions, chopped
½ cup (30 g) minced parsley leaves
8 slices prosciutto, minced
2 carrots, shredded
1 large leek, minced
1 teaspoon dried basil
2 teaspoons minced garlic
½ cup (75 g) butter
3 tablespoons (45 ml) olive oil
1 cup (70 g) finely chopped
    cabbage
3 tomatoes, peeled, diced,
    drained
3 small zucchini, diced
1½ cups (10 ounces) chicken
    stock
340 g (12 ounces) fusilli (spiral)
    pasta
⅓ cup (35 g) grated parmesan
    cheese

- Combine onions, parsley, prosciutto, carrots, leek, basil and garlic in bowl and mix well.

- Heat ¼ cup (60 g) butter and oil in large pot and stir in onion-carrot mixture. Cook on medium heat until onions and carrots are tender. Stir in cabbage, tomatoes, zucchini, stock and a little salt and pepper. Cover and simmer for 25 to 30 minutes.

- Cook pasta in saucepan according to package directions and drain. Place back into saucepan and stir in remaining butter. Toss until butter melts. Place pasta on heated serving platter and pour vegetable sauce over pasta. Sprinkle with parmesan cheese and serve hot. Serves 8 to 10.

Spice Up
the Spiral

**230 g (8 ounces) rotini
(spiral) pasta**
**⅓ cup (5½ tablespoons (75 g))
butter**
**230 g (8 ounces) shredded
processed cheese**
2 chopped green chillies
**1 280-g (10-ounce) can tomatoes
with liquid**
1 teaspoon paprika
½ onion, finely diced
230 g (8 ounces) sour cream

- Cook pasta in saucepan according to package directions, drain and add butter, stir until butter melts. Cover, set aside and keep warm.

- Preheat oven to 160° C (325° F).

- Combine cheese, paprika, tomatoes, green chillies and onion in large saucepan. Stir in pasta, heat on low for 5 minutes and stir occasionally.

- Fold in sour cream and pour into 2-L (2-quart) baking dish. Cover and bake for 20 minutes. Serves 8.

Fried Parmesan Pasta

455 g (16 ounces) farfalle (bow-tie) pasta
⅓ cup (75 ml) olive oil
3 tablespoons (45 ml) grated parmesan cheese
1 teaspoon onion powder
1 teaspoon garlic powder
1 teaspoon chilli powder

- Cook pasta in saucepan according to package directions, drain and rinse under cold water thoroughly.

- Heat oil in large frypan and fry individual pieces of pasta (about 1 cup/250 ml) at a time until golden. Drain in paper towels.

- Combine parmesan cheese, onion powder, garlic powder, chilli powder and ½ teaspoon salt in large bowl. Place fried pasta in bowl and toss until pasta coats with mixture. Serves 10 to 12.

Southwest Veggie Bake

230 g (8 ounces) rotelle (wagon wheels) pasta
2 455-g (16-ounce) jars hot, chunky salsa
230 g (8 ounces) shredded cheddar cheese
1 425-g (15-ounce) can chilli beans with liquid
1 425-g (15-ounce) can kidney beans, rinsed, drained
1 310-g (11-ounce) can corn kernels, drained
1 red capsicum, finely diced
1 cup (115 g) shredded mozzarella cheese

- Preheat oven to 175° C (350° F).

- Cook pasta in saucepan according to package directions and drain.

- Combine pasta, salsa, cheddar cheese, chilli beans, kidney beans, capsicum and corn in large bowl; mix well.

- Transfer to sprayed 23 x 33-cm (9 x 13-inch) baking dish. Cover and bake for 30 minutes. Uncover, top with mozzarella cheese and return to oven for 5 minutes. Serves 8 to 10.

Rotelle pasta is shaped like a wagon wheel and it means 'little wheels' in Italian.

Southwest Lasagna Rolls

425 g (15 ounces) ricotta cheese
1 cup (115 g) shredded mozzarella
    cheese
2 chopped green chillies
8 lasagna sheets
1 425-g (15-ounce) can lentils,
    drained
1 455-g (16-ounce) jar salsa

- Preheat oven to 175° C (350° F).

- Combine ricotta cheese, mozzarella cheese and green chillies in bowl and mix well.

- Cook lasagna sheets in saucepan according to package directions, drain and place on strip of baking paper. Spread cheese mixture on one side of each lasagna sheet. Carefully spoon lentils evenly over cheese mixture.

- Roll lasagna sheets and place, seam-side down on sprayed 18 x 28-cm (7 x 11-inch) baking dish. Spoon salsa over rolls, cover and bake for 25 minutes or until thoroughly hot. Serves 8.

A Fast Italian Fix

255 g (9 ounces) refrigerated
    wholemeal 4-cheese ravioli pasta
2 tablespoons (30 ml) olive oil
2 teaspoons minced garlic
230 g (½ pound) fresh green beans,
    ends snapped
2 yellow squash, quartered, sliced
½ cup (50 g) grated parmesan
    cheese

- Cook pasta in saucepan according to package directions, drain and keep warm.

- Heat oil in large frypan over medium-high heat and cook garlic for 1 minute. Add green beans and a little salt and pepper and cook, stirring often for 5 minutes.

- Add squash and cook for additional 5 minutes. Toss in pasta and cook on medium-low heat or until pasta is warm. Transfer to serving bowl and sprinkle cheese over top. Serve immediately. Serves 8.

Spinach Lover's Lasagna

455 g (16 ounces) cottage cheese
3 eggs, beaten
2 280-g (10-ounce) packages
    frozen chopped
    spinach, thawed,
    drained
1 teaspoon minced garlic
1 740-g (26-ounce) jar chunky
    vegetable spaghetti sauce
9 cooked lasagna sheets
230 g (8 ounces) shredded
    mozzarella cheese
¼ cup (45 g) plus 3 tablespoons
    grated parmesan cheese

- Preheat oven at 175° C (350° F).

- Combine cottage cheese, eggs, spinach and garlic in medium bowl; set aside.

- Spread ½ cup (125 ml) spaghetti sauce in sprayed 23 x 33-cm (9 x 13-inch) baking dish.

- Place 3 lasagna sheets over sauce; spoon one-third spinach mixture over lasagna sheets. Top with one-third remaining spaghetti sauce, ½ cup (60 g) mozzarella and 3 tablespoons (45 ml) parmesan.

- Repeat layers twice with remaining lasagna sheets, spinach mixture, spaghetti sauce, 1 cup (115 g) mozzarella and remaining parmesan cheese. Top with remaining mozzarella cheese.

- Bake for 35 minutes or until bubbly around edges of dish. Let stand for 10 minutes before serving. Serves 8.

Capsicum Topped Ravioli

**510 g (18 ounces) refrigerated
cheese-filled ravioli pasta**
¼ cup (60 ml) olive oil
1 onion, chopped
**1 large green capsicum,
seeded, julienned**
**1 large red capsicum,
seeded, julienned**
2 cups (500 ml) chicken stock
⅛ teaspoon cayenne pepper

- Cook pasta in saucepan according to package directions and drain. Transfer to serving bowl and keep warm.

- Heat oil in frypan over medium heat. Sauté onion and capsicums until tender, stirring often. Stir in 1 cup (250 ml) chicken stock and season with a little salt and cayenne pepper.

- Cook on medium heat for 5 to 6 minutes. Stir in remaining stock and continue cooking until most of liquid has evaporated. Spoon capsicum mixture over pasta and serve hot. Serves 3 to 4.

Ravioli is a filled pasta. It has two layers of pasta pressed together with fillings such as meat, cheese or mushrooms. It is commonly cooked by boiling and is served with a sauce.

Wholemeal Ravioli Toss

510 g (18 ounces) wholemeal cheese-
  filled ravioli pasta
2 tablespoons (30 ml) olive oil
1 tablespoon (15 ml) minced garlic
280 g (10 ounces) frozen cut green
  beans, thawed
2 yellow squash, quartered, sliced
1 red capsicum, seeded, chopped
¾ cup (85 g) shredded romano
  cheese

- Cook pasta in saucepan according
  to package directions, drain and
  place in large serving bowl.
  Keep warm.

- Heat oil in large frypan and cook
  garlic, green beans, squash and
  capsicum for 5 to 7 minutes or until
  vegetables are tender. Stir often.

- Transfer to bowl with pasta, add
  a little salt and pepper and toss.
  Sprinkle with cheese and serve
  immediately. Serves 8 to 10.

Creamy Spinach Pasta

200 g (7 ounces) refrigerated cheese-
  filled spinach tortellini pasta
8 slices bacon, cooked, crumbled
¼ cup (15 g) chopped fresh parsley
1 roasted red capsicum chopped,
  drained
½ cup (50 g) grated parmesan
  cheese
Dash of cayenne pepper
⅔–¾ cup (160–180 g) sour cream
3 fresh spring onions,
  thinly sliced

- Cook pasta in saucepan according
  to package directions, drain and
  place in bowl. Stir in crumbled
  bacon, parsley, roasted red
  capsicum, cheese, cayenne pepper
  and a little salt; mix well.

- Add sour cream in small amounts
  until mixture is moist but not
  soggy. Top with spring onions.
  Serves 4.

Nutty Stir-Fry Tortellini

255 g (9 ounces) refrigerated mixed cheese-filled tortellini pasta
455 g (16 ounces) frozen stir-fry vegetables, thawed
1 red capsicum, seeded, julienned
2 tablespoons (30 ml) olive oil
¾ cup (175 ml) peanut stir-fry sauce
⅓ cup (45 g) chopped dry-roasted cashews

- Cook pasta in saucepan according to package directions, drain and set aside. Stir-fry mixed vegetables and capsicums in large frypan with oil over medium-high heat for 5 to 6 minutes or until tender but crisp.

- Add pasta, stir-fry sauce and toss gently to coat well. Heat thoroughly and sprinkle with cashews. Serve immediately. Serves 4.

TIP: Frozen stir-fry vegetables may vary so if capsicums are included, choose a different second vegetable.

Tortellini is a filled pasta. Usually a circle of pasta is used with a filling of cheese or meat placed on half of the pasta. The pasta is then folded over, sealed, and twisted into a ring. It is cooked in boiling water and served with a sauce.

Italian Tortellini

510 g (18 ounces) refrigerated
    cheese-filled tortellini pasta
455 g (16 ounces) frozen broccoli
    florets, thawed
¾ cup (40 g) drained, chopped
    sun-dried tomatoes in oil
2½ cups (630 g) pasta sauce
3 tablespoons (45 g) butter, melted
¾ cup (90 g) breadcrumbs
1 teaspoon Italian seasoning

- Preheat oven to 175° C (350° F).

- Cook pasta in large saucepan according to package directions, drain and return to saucepan.

- Stir in broccoli, tomatoes, pasta sauce and spoon into 23 x 33-cm (9 x 13-inch) baking dish.

- Combine melted butter and breadcrumbs and seasoning in small bowl and sprinkle over top.

- Bake for 30 minutes. Serves 8.

Savoury Spinach Tortellini

2 tablespoons (30 ml) olive oil
1 teaspoon minced garlic
1 small onion, finely chopped
2 425-g (15-ounce) cans Italian
    stewed tomatoes
1 tablespoon (15 ml) sugar
400 g (14 ounces) spinach tortellini
    pasta with cheese

- Heat oil in large frypan and sauté garlic and onion; do not brown. Stir in stewed tomatoes and sugar. Bring to a boil, reduce heat and simmer on medium-low for about 30 minutes or until it thickens.

- Cook pasta in saucepan according to package directions, drain and rinse. Transfer pasta to serving bowl and spoon tomato sauce over top. Serve immediately.
Serves 4 to 6.

Unforgettable Tortellini Bake

510 g (18 ounces) refrigerated cheese tortellini pasta, cooked, drained
455 g (16 ounces) frozen chopped broccoli florets, thawed, drained
1 roasted red capsicum, sliced
1 onion, chopped
1 capsicum, seeded, chopped
2 280-g (10-ounce) cans cream of chicken soup
1 teaspoon minced garlic
1 teaspoon Italian seasoning
230 g (8 ounces) shredded mozzarella cheese

- Preheat oven to 175° C (350° F).

- Combine pasta, broccoli, roasted red capsicum, onion, capsicum, soup, garlic and Italian seasoning in large bowl. Mix well. Fold in half cheese and pour into sprayed 3-L (3-quart) baking dish. Cover and bake for 45 minutes.

- Remove from oven, sprinkle remaining cheese over top and return to oven for 5 minutes. Serves 8.

Bubbling Butternut Pumpkin and Orzo

**680 g (1½ pounds) butternut
   pumpkin, peeled, seeded,
   cubed**
230 g (8 ounces) mushrooms, halved
1 onion, cut in thin wedges
1 teaspoon dried oregano
2 tablespoons (30 ml) olive oil
**1 litre (14 ounces) chicken
   stock**
230 g (8 ounces) orzo (tiny) pasta
1 teaspoon minced garlic
**½ cup (65 g) chopped walnuts,
   toasted**

- Preheat oven to 205° C (400° F).

- Place pumpkin pieces in sprayed
  25 x 38-cm (10 x 15-inch) baking
  pan. Sprinkle with lots of black
  pepper, cover and bake for
  10 minutes.

- Uncover and add mushrooms,
  onion, oregano and oil; toss.
  Return to oven and roast for
  15 minutes or until vegetables
  are tender and light brown,
  stirring often.

- Bring stock in large saucepan to
  a boil, reduce heat and keep stock
  simmering. Spray frypan over
  medium heat and add pasta and
  garlic; cook, stirring often, for
  about 3 minutes or until pasta is
  light brown. Remove from heat.

- Stir in ½ cup (125 ml) hot stock
  and return to heat. Cook, stirring
  often, until liquid absorbs.
  Continue adding stock to pasta,
  ½ cup (125 ml) at a time and
  cook until liquid absorbs before
  adding more. Stir each time.
  Pasta will need about 15 minutes
  cooking time.

- Add roasted vegetables and
  walnuts to pasta mixture and stir
  well. Serves 4.

Confetti Orzo

¾ cup (80 g) orzo (tiny) pasta
½ cup (115 g) butter
340 g (12 ounces) frozen
    broccoli florets, thawed
1 bunch fresh spring onions,
    chopped
1 red capsicum, seeded,
    chopped
1 green capsicum, seeded,
    chopped
2 teaspoons minced garlic
2 chicken stock cubes
1 455-g (16-ounce) jar creamy
    alfredo sauce

- Preheat oven to 160° C (325° F).

- Cook pasta in saucepan according to package directions. Drain. Cook butter, broccoli, onions, capsicums and garlic in large frypan on medium heat for 10 to 15 minutes, until tender but crisp.

- Spoon into large bowl, combine broccoli mixture, pasta, chicken stock cubes and alfredo sauce and mix well. Cover and bake for 30 minutes. If you like, add 3 cups (420 g) cooked, cubed chicken to casserole. Serves 6.

While some consider couscous a pasta because it is made from semolina and water, purists tend to consider it a separate type of food. It is grain-shaped and is sometimes mistaken for a grain. Originally from North Africa, it is increasingly popular in Australia.

Mushroom Pasta

1 onion, chopped
1 cup (100 g) celery, chopped
1 green capsicum, seeded,
    chopped
1 red capsicum, seeded,
    chopped
6 tablespoons (90 g) butter
1⅓ cups (140 g) orzo (tiny) pasta
½ litre (14 ounces) beef stock
1 200-g (7-ounce) can sliced
    mushrooms, drained
1 tablespoon (15 ml) Worcestershire
    sauce
¾ cup (95 g) chopped walnuts
Chopped spring onions

- Preheat oven to 160° C (325° F).

- Sauté onion, celery and capsicums with butter in frypan.

- Cook pasta in beef stock and 1 cup (250 ml) water in saucepan for 10 to 11 minutes and drain.

- Combine onion-capsicum mixture, pasta, mushrooms, Worcestershire sauce, walnuts and ½ teaspoon each of salt and pepper in large bowl and mix well.

- Transfer to sprayed 2-L (2-quart) baking dish. Cover and bake for 30 minutes.

- When ready to serve, sprinkle chopped spring onions over top of casserole. Serves 6.

Orzo Bake

340 g (12 ounces) orzo (tiny) pasta
¼ cup (60 g) butter, melted
300 g (1 pint) cherry tomatoes,
    halved
½ cup (75 g) diced green
    capsicum
1¼ cups (145 g) shredded
    mozzarella cheese
½ cup (125 ml) white cooking wine
1 teaspoon minced garlic
1 tablespoon (15 ml) dried parsley

- Preheat oven to 175° C (350° F).

- Cook pasta in saucepan according to package directions and drain.

- Combine pasta, butter, cherry tomatoes, capsicum, ¾ cup (85 g) cheese, wine, garlic, parsley and a little salt and pepper in bowl.

- Transfer to sprayed 2-L (2-quart) baking dish. Cover and bake for about 20 minutes. Uncover and sprinkle remaining cheese over top of casserole. Serves 8.

Spinach-Orzo Bake

340 g (12 ounces) frozen
    spinach quiche, crust removed
455 g (16 ounces) orzo
    (tiny) pasta
2 tablespoons (30 ml) olive oil
½ cup (70 g) roasted red capsicum,
    drained
1 teaspoon paprika
½ cup (60 g) shredded mozzarella
    cheese

- Cook spinach quiche in microwave according to package directions.

- Cook pasta in saucepan according to package directions, transfer to large bowl and stir in olive oil.

- Add quiche, paprika and roasted red capsicum; mix well. Transfer to sprayed 2-L (2-quart) baking dish. Cover with mozzarella cheese. Serve immediately or cover and heat for 10 minutes at 160° C (325° F). Serves 4.

Fancy Green Beans

910 g (32 ounces) frozen
    French-style green
    beans, thawed
½ cup (115 g) butter
230 g (8 ounces) fresh mushrooms,
    sliced
2 280-g (10-ounce) cans cream
    of chicken soup
⅔ cup (90 g) sliced roasted red
    capsicum
2 teaspoons (10 ml) soy sauce
1 cup (115 g) shredded
    cheddar cheese
⅔ cup (90 g) chopped cashews
⅔ cup (40 g) chow mein noodles

- Preheat oven to 160° C (325° F).

- Cook green beans in saucepan according to package directions, drain and set aside. Melt butter in large saucepan and sauté mushrooms for about 5 minutes, but do not brown.

- Stir in soups, ¼ cup (60 ml) water, roasted red capsicum, soy sauce and cheese and gently mix.

- Fold in drained green beans and spoon into sprayed 23 x 33-cm (9 x 13-inch) baking pan.

- Combine cashews and noodles in bowl, sprinkle over top of casserole and bake for 30 minutes or until edges are hot and bubbly. Serves 10 to 12.

Quick Glance Pasta Chart

Category	Italian Name	English Name/Description
Strands	spaghetti	different size strands
	vermicelli	thin spaghetti
	capelli d'angelo	angel hair
Stickbons	tagliatelle	thin egg noodles
	margherite	narrow egg noodles
	linguine	thin egg noodles (⅛ inch)
	fettuccini	medium egg noodles (¼ inch)
	pappardelle	wide egg noodles (⅝ inch)
Sheet	lasagna	very wide; sometimes fluted edges
Tubes	macaroni	different size tubes
	elbow macaroni	curved tubes
	ditali	short tubes
	penne	tubes cut diagonally
	mostaccioli	little moustaches
	ziti	thin tubes
	rigatoni	large tubes
	manicotti	large tubes
	gigantoni	extra large tubes

continued next page…

Quick Glance Pasta Chart – continued

Category	Italian Name	English Name/Description
Bow-ties	farfalle	butterfly pasta; bow-tie pasta
	tripolini	small bow-ties
Shells	cavatelli	short with ridges
	conchiglie	conch shells
	maruzze	seashells
	lumache	large shell
Spirals	fusilli	spiral spaghetti (1½ inches long)
	rotini	short spirals (1 inch long)
	cavatappi	corkscrew pasta
Other Shapes	rotelle	wagon wheels
	stelline	stars
	orzo	small rice-shaped pasta
	riso	small rice-shaped pasta
	pastina	tiny dough balls
	tortellini	ring-shaped, usually filled (with cheese or meat)
	genelli	twisted
	ravioli	square-shaped, filled pasta
	gnocchi	dumplings made with potato or flour

Index

I

K

L

M

N

O

P

W

Y

Z